INNER GLOW

A Modern Woman's Guide to Spirituality

Gemma Stower
with Jo Withey

Contents

About me and why I have written this book.

Many universities and Ivy League colleges have proven that as a society, we have become attached to financial status and material gain; we have slowly moved away from the power of savouring moments, of random acts of kindness and sharing experiences.

We become so focused on the next thing, the next new upgrade, a newer model car, a better body, a bigger house, we only briefly admire and recognise these "accomplishments" and then it's onto the next round. These things, however, never bring us the joy we think they will, they just take our time, energy, and focus away from the present.

I, for one, have been extremely guilty of this. I believed I loved, deserved, and needed these expensive things as a reward for my intense job; a job I often spent seventy hours a week nurturing. As a result, I was always looking for the next pay rise or promotion, my compensation for the exchange of time and effort. Truthfully, I measured my value on my input. Gosh, I laugh now, that I used to treat having to get up at 4.30am on a Monday to run a report, as some badge of honour. I would constantly be available to my large team and to my boss. Both phones would always be in my hands, even sharing my bed. The first thing I would do in the morning would be accessing my emails. I couldn't even see (my glasses crew know what's up), I would squint at my phone, allowing anxiety or even anger to wash over me, seeing that one of my sites had not made financial targets, or a task had not been completed. My mind was already racing with what I had to "achieve" that day. Imagine that was how I would choose to start my day, every day.

I would then spend the day buried in my phone or laptop. More often than not, I was distracted in personal conversations, never present in the joys of day-to-day life. I would cancel self-care, gym sessions, and events with friends because I would become so drained from the effort I dedicated to my job. I benchmarked my success with materials. I would spend spare time wondering what I would buy with my next bonus, or which country to visit. I truly believed I was happy, I loved my job, my team, I had great relationships with my bosses, and I was having a positive impact in my work life, yeah, I was stressed, but that's because I was in a high-profile role. That is what I chose to do. I held the belief that everyone should dedicate their time to their careers like I did. I embarrassingly questioned others who didn't seem as focused on success, I couldn't understand why someone would choose to work part time, when their schedule would allow them to do full time, why were they not working on their education, or on their next promotion? Didn't they want more from life?

I get it now; I fully get it.

Like many, the company I was working for went into liquidation in 2020. I had been off work on furlough for a few months already, and I knew the company wouldn't survive, so this didn't come as a shock. I had loved the break from the hectic lifestyle. I missed my vibrant city of London, but not the commute. I certainly didn't miss the stress of choosing the right outfit every morning – the outfit that would seem professional, and approachable, rather than "too sexy or fashionable", and most importantly, one that felt flattering on the days I felt bloated. I certainly don't miss coming home to piles of clothes on the bed when I just couldn't decide what to wear. I am kinder to my body now – even though I went up a dress size – because now I dress for myself in the morning, what colour or fabric feels attractive to *me*. I loved having time to enjoy my home, to have time to explore being creative – heads up, I'm not, but I enjoy it. I liked the slower pace.

The moment I realised I didn't want to return to my previous lifestyle came when I was offered a great role with an international company, a fancy title and a six-figure salary. My ego wanted the job title, the old me wanted the income, the new me felt disengaged. I turned the role down. My poor husband, although supportive, rightfully questioned my decision; was I sure I didn't want to just try it, or do it until the pandemic was over? Nope, I did not. Intuition told me it was the right choice, even with a lack of logic to support it. I turned down the role to teach yoga and be a life coach, in the middle of lockdown and a recession.

I know I made the right decision. That change allowed me to step back and reflect, to practice gratitude, to get to know my higher self, to find space and inner peace. The most wonderful thing is, these days I walk downstairs, pop the kettle on for my decaf coffee, old habits die hard, I step onto my patio, and I admire the day, whatever the weather, and I practice gratitude. Small things that I feel blessed about. It's a morning routine I highly recommend.

I now spend my days helping busy professionals and athletes find their inner peace.

I am by no means suggesting you quit your job and make a drastic change in your career.

I am here to simply share insight I wish I had back then. I wish someone had held my hand, guided me through practices, or just simply slapped me in the face. I needed it. This book shares ways to bring spirituality to your already busy schedule, giving you the chance to connect to your higher self and find inner peace. I want to help you love yourself, to honour your downtime, to practice compassion and healthy boundaries, helping you thrive at work and at home.

I am positive this book will provide guidance, so that you can not only recognise what causes you anxiety and what brings you inner peace, but also how you can create a world and a life that you feel honoured to be lead role in. You can be the CEO, you can start the business, you can want the career, the house, the success in life, and still feel connected and aligned to your values. This book shares ways to unlock your potential by freeing up your mind from the constant chatter and self-doubt, creating space and clarity to succeed where you need. It will help you be present in your journey so that you are profoundly grateful for this wondrous life you have carved for yourself.

I want to help you find bliss. You deserve it, you are worthy, and you are divine.

Alas, I am not so fabulous as to be able to do this without help. As well as lessons and tools I have gathered from teachers, mentors, leaders, friends, science journals, books, podcasts, and inspirational yoga classes, I asked my dear friend to help me. The one and only Jo, or Jo head kick, as she is saved in my phone.

I met Jo in our MMA gym, instant love. I was reluctant to meet her, our coach had been raving about each of us, to the other, for a while. Every time I went there, Chris would say that I need to meet Jo, that he thinks we would get on blah blah blah. Truthfully, I thought he just wanted us to meet as there's a lack of females in combat gyms, and from what I could tell, she was in my weight category. So, in my clouded judgment, I believed Chris was just happy he had found someone I could spar with. There's a lot of unfounded female rivalry in gyms, I am sure I don't need to explain. We have all been in situations where we have been pitted against another woman, rather than shown how to support her.

Well, I was wrong, Chris was right. I finally met Jo in a Muay Thai class. Instantly I had this profound respect for the fierce woman kicking me in my head. Yup. Here she was trying to kick my head off, as much as you can in a controlled spar setting, and I had this strange sense of admiration. I had never enjoyed sparring with a woman so much. Rather than anger when a shot was landed, there was a nod of appreciation. We had created a space for us both to learn and evolve our technique. We had a little chat after class, shared the same positive experience and swapped numbers. Within days we were sharing outrageous memes and planning to hang out, outside of the gym. This vibrant, colourful, creative, feminine creature quickly became a great friend. Back then I was still doing my thing working in the city, whilst Jo was running her own business, making stunning boho style wedding dresses and competition outfits for pole dancers. I loved that she made the bold decision to turn her back on the London fashion scene to honour her own creations. It was Jo's braveness that gave me the confidence to eventually do the same. Jo is my hype girl, the one that through witty one liners and hysterical tales of her five-year-old, constantly kept me out of my comfort zone, and rolling around on the floor, grateful we both only have tears running down our face, and not down our legs, my mama's know what's up. The first time she led me out of my comfort zone, she encouraged me to enter a kickboxing tournament. I just need to share with you, I was past the age of thirty, and had only found the sport that same year. My fitness was maybe a little above average. Anyway, I did the event, with her cheering me on from the side. I got a cool trophy and learnt a lot about myself that day. After that, Jo asked me to assist her at a fashion event. Wearing one of the pole outfits, not the wedding dresses. She would bespoke one of her designs, using more material than usual, so I felt covered enough. Of course I agreed to help her, sales and chatting to customers is my thang! We had a great day, so when the next event came around, naturally I jumped at the chance to help again. I didn't think to ask what my outfit would be. On the day, once we had set up the stall, JoJo presented me with a Britney-esq outfit complete with a white feather tail. Such a spectacular outfit! Normally it would be an outright no. I felt hesitant, but well, I just wanted to support my great friend, so on it went. After an hour, the embarrassment of not wearing very much in a room full of people, mostly in a typical Saturday jeans and T-shirt combo, disappeared. It came back with a vengeance when I clocked the girl from accounts that worked in my head office. The sighting was never mentioned by said accountant, but we both know she saw me. The world didn't end. So, when Jo asked if I would enter a pole dancing competition with her, it didn't cross my mind to say no, even though I had never done anything other than a singular groupon pole class. The competition was a few months away, I had time to learn. I made it to almost eight pole classes by the day of the competition, but you know what, I wasn't scared. Jo and I didn't win, as you can imagine, we got some cool medals, a load of great photos, and hours of belly laughter in the rehearsals.

Reading this back it might sound like my mate leads me down eccentric paths ha-ha, she is the opposite, she is the kindest soul, she's in tune with her values, she has a super holistic approach to life and applies it in a refreshingly modern way. Jo taught me what happens outside my comfort zone, in that uncomfortable place where we learn a lot about who we are under pressure. She showed me that you can make a female friend in your 30's and fiercely champion everything they do, without jealousy. Jo taught me the world doesn't end with these moments we catastrophize in our heads, that you are never too old to pivot direction, find a new passion, wear tiny pants on stage in a room full of strangers, laugh until you wee a little – her, not me. That it doesn't matter how professional (and whatever the opposite of hippy is) you think you are, there's a benefit to hearing someone you trust talk about the power of the body healing itself, how hypnotherapy works, why you gotta un-block your chakra, and how you can safely hold a baby over a sink to poop, if you don't want to change a nappy.

So here Jo is, stepping outside her comfort zone and shar-ing not only her incredible insight in some of these chapters, but also for getting her art kit back out and creating bewitch-ing illustrations for this book, even though she's held onto a negative comment from her college art teacher for the past ten years, who told her she wasn't any good.

Fuck that teacher. Fuck everyone who taught you to think negative thoughts about your beautiful self, fuck the opinion that you can't have it all, fuck the notion you must settle for feeling mediocre, or that stress and anxiety can't do one. Fuck the weirdo's who don't champion your jour-ney to getting to know the best version of you. Fuck not being peaceful daily. Fuck anything and anyone that holds you back from the blissful life you deserve.

This book is created for the modern woman, whatever your wants and desires.

Meet Jo.

Much like Gem, I fell into the trap of feeling perpetually stressed being part of the rat race. At the time, I just couldn't see the wood for the trees. I worked as a Garment Tech-nologist for a high street fashion supplier – a job I loved but found extremely stressful.

A turning point for me was when my body sent me a very firm message to slow the fuck down before I made myself seriously ill. I had been rushing to a meeting, which I was absolutely dreading; I was really feeling the pres-sure from my company and the client over a pleated pair of trousers. I had to jump off the bus on Oxford Street – my heart was pounding; I was as white as a sheet and I was sweating. Struggling to catch my breath, I dived into one of the department stores and asked for a cup of water. At this point I was in a blind state of panic, this sounds overly dramatic, but I was actually convinced I was about to die.

So, that was my first panic attack. I pulled myself together and carried on running to the meeting. The work problem was solved, but I had been given quite a wakeup call. Over the next few weeks, I continued to suffer from heart palpitations, and I eventually saw my GP. I do suffer from white coat syndrome which was exacerbated by my Dad having had a suspected heart attack a few years prior, so when the Doctor checked me my blood pressure was through the roof. I was referred for ECG's. I remember laying there being monitored and feeling my heart pounding, the tests had put me in the same state of stress. I was diagnosed with an irregular heartbeat and prescribed Beta Blockers.

I can't explain why, but something stopped me from taking that medication. The diagnosis just felt wrong. Although I was terrified that I may have had a serious health condition, something was telling me there had to be another way without reaching for medication. I started to look at breathing techniques, lowered my caffeine and alcohol intake, and began to make more time for things I used to enjoy such as exercise and reading.

I managed my stress levels slightly better in the following years but being at work for twelve hours a day just wasn't how I wanted to live my life. I'm not sure why I did it for as long as I did, I moved to a higher paid position within another company, but it was one in which you could just sense the stress levels. A few days in and I knew I would never be happy there. I had been making dance costumes and wedding dresses as a side hustle for a few years, so I decided at that point to leave my full-time position to really push on with that whilst freelancing as a Technical Manager – it gave me the ideal work life balance.

At that point I became pregnant. I was thrilled and

absolutely terrified in equal measure. I had always been frightened of birth, the dramatic labours I had seen on television and traumatic birth stories people told were my only reference point at the time. In desperation I began searching YouTube for hypnobirths, I couldn't believe my eyes – watching strong powerful mothers calmly, and meditatively, breathing out their baby.

Free of medical intervention and shockingly – free of pain!

I knew I had to learn more. I booked onto a hypnobirthing course at the hospital, but this wouldn't commence until much later in my pregnancy. I knew I needed all the practice I could get at being calm and letting go, so I ordered a book and began listening to the hypnosis tracks. They were so calming and beautiful. I joined a prenatal Yoga class which was just the most wonderful experience, the movements and breathwork perfectly complemented the hypnobirthing techniques I had been learning. The classes closed with beautiful relaxations that included visualising your baby which made me feel so connected to the miracle growing inside me.

Giving birth was the most amazing, life changing experience. I had a wonderful water birth; I had planned to do so at home but was transferred to hospital for dehydration. There was one point in the labour that I lost myself and became distressed. They were monitoring the baby and called in a consultant and my mind was pulled out of the present moment and zoomed off into a vortex of 'what if' – the panic and pain hit me like a bus! I don't think there could possibly have been a clearer demonstration of the power of the mind and body connection for me than that. I was about to demand all of the drugs, but my husband calmly stepped in and reminded me to focus on my breathing and stay calm.

I am so grateful to have learnt those techniques, and I've used them in other situations to stay calm and pain free. Perfect for the dentist or a bikini wax!

I am very aware of how emotions directly affect our physiology, so I am grateful to have my spirituality practices. Since the birth of my son, I have wanted to explore spirituality more and more, it is important to me to lead by example – to show him my true self, complete with my weaknesses and my strengths. To teach him that all emotions and feelings are valid and should be faced openly and honestly.

I really believe that exploring and nurturing your inner glow is the key to a happy and fulfilling life, and I hope we are able to help you on your journey.

Spirituality

History of Spirituality

What even is Spirituality?

noun
1. The quality of being concerned with the human spirit or soul as opposed to material or physical things.

"The shift in priorities allows us to embrace our spirituality in a more profound way."

Definition from Oxford Languages.
Spirituality can mean many things to many people. Its meaning has developed and grown over time and can have many different connotations.

More traditionally, spirituality refers to the religious process of 'reformation', which is the ultimate goal to "recover the original shape of man" free of mortal sin' and in the image of God.

But what does Spirituality mean today?

The term has spread widely into other religious traditions, making it more relevant to a wider audience with a wider range of experience.

A huge influence on modern spirituality was the Theosophical Society, who sought to uncover the 'secret teachings' in Asian Religions.

Following the Second World War spirituality became increasingly oriented on subjective experience and a desire to reach an expression of the true self through free expression and meditation rather than by conforming to theistic religious expectations.

This distinction between spiritual and religious became more distinct with the rise of the New Age Movement.

A BRIEF HISTORY OF
SPIRITUALITY

noun
1. The quality of being concerned with the human spirit or soul as opposed to material or physical things.
Oxford dictionary

5TH CENTURY

First evidence of the word "spirituality" 5th century and by the end of the middle ages, the term was in common use. In the original biblical context, the term literally meant, "being animated by God", referring to the concept of living a life driven by the Holy Spirit.

11TH CENTURY

The meaning of the word, began to evolve to denote the mental aspect of life, as opposed to more material aspects.

13TH CENTURY

Spirituality acquired a social status. Socially it referred to the domain of the clergy vs the secular classes.

13TH CENTURY

Spirituality began to take form as, "the realm of the inner life". This practice is one we have come to know and love today. It refers to intrinsic practice of turning inwards, analysing feelings, the purity of motives, affections, intentions, inner dispositions, and the psychology of living a spiritual life.

17TH-18TH CENTURY

the term acquired more negative social connotations, gradually becoming widely linked with mysticism. Distinctions were also starting to be made between higher and lower levels of spirituality, for example people started to claim that to be 'Spiritual' you must be more Christian than the next person

19TH-20TH CENTURY

Christian ideals started to integrate with Western esoteric traditions. It is in this time period, that spirituality became more distinct and disconnected from traditional religious organisations

19TH CENTURY

Transcendentalism was an early 19th century liberal Protestant movement pioneered by Ralph Waldo Emerson (1803-1882). Transcendentalists practiced an intuitive, experiential approach to religion. In the late 18th century, the first translations of Hindu texts started to appear and began to influence Transcendentalists. They also endorsed Unitarian Universalism, believing there must be truth in other religions as a loving God would redeem all living creatures, not just Christians.
A huge influence on modern spirituality was the Theosophical Society, who sought to uncover the 'secret teachings' in Asian Religions.

1945

Following the Second World War spirituality became increasingly oriented on subjective experience and a desire to reach an expression of the true self through free expression and meditation rather than by conforming to theistic religious expectations.

The word "spiritual" originates from the Latin word "spiritus" meaning, breath, soul, or life. It is often articulated as being concerned with the human spirit or soul rather than materialistic possessions. Yet most people don't really understand what it encompasses, or more so, what it does not. Even before I started this book, I was interested in others' opinion of the word spirituality, especially at the start of my journey. Upon reflection, I can see that asking this question was my way of feeling safe to explore this "thing" that I held a distorted opinion of for so many years, that suddenly, I felt drawn to. I needed guidance, reassurance, and information, to feel authentic as I started on this path. For the start of my adult life, I held a view that what I learned was quite common amongst others. Oh, you know the one. The stereotype. Yup, that one. The prejudice that it was hippies doing mushrooms, au natural, frolicking in flowy dresses with wild hair, sticking it to the man, shunning traditions to be bums in communes – cool, but not for me. Obviously, that's no longer my opinion, although I definitely see the appeal in some of the above. I found many others held similar views. Spirituality is also often poo pooed, as it can be viewed as religious and that's always a topic that can get peoples backs up, or instantly turn them off. I strongly believe that it is mostly seen as extreme ways and beliefs that seem so disconnected from your current world, that we end up rejecting the whole idea. For me this was certainly the case. My old view had me believing spirituality was smoking weed, playing with crystals, visiting psychics, and hanging dream catchers and tie dye curtains. That was not too far removed from my world of business meetings, designer bags and my neutral colours only, farrow and ball decorated home. Truthfully, none of these things are currently in my spiritual journey. This is not to be disrespectful to those who partake, I just identify easier with other aspects. At the start of my journey,

I noticed I was sometimes embarrassed to share these new interests I had, I would start statements with "I know it sounds weird." ... It's not that I was embarrassed about meditating for example, it was almost a reluctance to admit it, as if I were being disrespectful to the old me, who could never sit still. There was a little worry that these people who have known me for 15/20 years, would call me out as fake or stop liking me. Who was the authentic me? The old me who hated silence and stillness, or this new me who vibes out to the sound of nature? Could I be both? Those two lifestyles seemed so far apart. How could I be a person who felt confident delivering budget meetings to board members, and yet the same person that wanted to be barefoot and feel connected to the earth? This juxta-position had me questioning myself, as well as the things I had been coveting. Could I be spiritual and still have spa days and cute outfits. So many things to reflect on. Most importantly where did I, and so many others, accumulate this poor opinion of a spiritual journey?

It was interesting to see just who around me considered themselves spiritual, who held a dismissive view of spirit-uality, and who just didn't really know what it meant to be spiritual. There was nothing visibly noticeable for those around me on their own journey, no common recognisable factor. Not a uniform, a cult tattoo, or particular style even. In fact, many spiritual people in my life wear a suit daily. The only common factor I can say they all had, was an air of confidence – not arrogance or anything down that gross road, but a vibe, that you just know they are ok with who they are, and what's going on around them. Almost like they're in on a big secret, as if they know how it all pans out, and there's no resistance to the outcome. Have you ever seen a funny prank play out, and you can tell who knew the details, as they reacted with acceptance, rather than the blind panic you might expect? A *what will be will be* sensation. These spiritual souls are very much like that. I must note, that accepting feeling I picked up on was never due to them not caring, it wasn't a lack of giving a shit, it was like a cool state of entertained calm. They glide through life, caring and happy, contributing to society and their community. They experience the same annoying, stressful, sad things that we all do, they just bounce back easier, they don't seem to hold things in their heart so much, they seem to display more patience and compassion for others around them. They also have a great sense of awareness of who they are. A lot of them reported feeling connected, either to themselves, or the world around them; knowing and feeling comforted by the awareness that they are just a tiny speck in the universe, a drop in the ocean, dust in the wind.

Sadly, I found too many with the opinion that to be spiritual meant eating lentils and feeling superior to others. Displaying signs of superiority to others, due to a lack of beliefs or behaviours, is a sign of an untamed ego, not a spiritual person. A person who, for example, practices meditation as part of their journey yet uses opportunities to belittle others who may not meditate, is someone struggling to manage their ego. Treat them with kindness, they're still working on their own demons. Please don't let it put you off your own soul journey.

Naturally, there is a blurred viewpoint of spirituality being religious or meaning a belief in a higher power in the form of a God, or many Gods.

You can be both spiritual and religious, however, you can also be spiritual and an atheist.

There are crossovers between the two, a craving for a deeper meaning and connection, an awe of divinity, both have communities, and both are lifestyles.

In Religion you are given rules to abide by, yet being spiritual means acting with your own moral compass and personal knowledge of what's right. Spirituality is an internal journey; religion is a dictated path. Spirituality is your authentic self; religion is the conditioned self.

Wait, so what the F is spirituality?

I will share what my current perception of spirituality is. I imagine one day I will read this and my perspective will again have shifted and evolved.

For me, at this stage of my journey, being spiritual is a deep sense of comfort knowing that I have a place in the universe, that I am always on the right path, and that I have what I need within me. A strong desire to connect to my soul and my body, creating space to move freely and then settle into stillness. A feeling of overwhelming gratitude, which is always extensively exaggerated by nature, in particular the ocean and the moon. A desire to be less influenced by expensive things, this has been exchanged for desires of experiences, and an inclination to be more present, even for the mundane moments. Taking time to turn inwards, to really get to know me, so that I can evolve, working on becoming my higher self, my most authentic me, rather than only focusing on developing personal growth to attain the next promotion or status.

Higher self

Your higher self is the best version of you that you can possibly be. No, not the most groomed, polished, beautiful you, accepting the business award whilst ticking off all of society's traditions, by buying a house and getting married, not that one. Your higher self is the purest, most truthful version of you. It's the you after you shed the titles you have been awarded so far, no longer a daughter, a sister, a girlfriend, a wife, the role you adopted within your group of friends, no longer represented by your job title. Now shed all the things that you have been taught and conditioned to desire, all the ways you have been told how to behave. The higher you, is not defined by your outfit, or how you look. Your higher self is compassionate and full of love, your higher self is connected to the cosmos, it's your soul, it doesn't covet belongings, or a status, and it doesn't want to control people. Your higher self simply *is*. It's a blissful state, and it wants others to find the same harmony within.

Your higher self is wise and will guide you safely. It knows that life is a gift, and everything is a lesson.

Connecting to your higher self may mean curiously questioning the things you were raised expected to believe. Your higher self's purpose may not be aligned with the status quo. You will need to release your ego and learn to listen to, and honour, your intuition. You will need to be prepared to be radically honest about the traits of your lower self. We all have a lower self, with varying habits and responses. Our lower self can be identified as our ego. Oh, how many times has your ego got in your way, stopping you from trying something, from enjoying something, from feeling content. Ego is "I", your higher self or your soul comes from a place of "we". Your ego craves recognition and validation, your higher self values inner peace and alignment to your values.

Ego	Soul
Power	Unity
Jealousy	Love
War	Forgiveness
Feels superior	Feels humble
Self-separation	Connection
Judges	Has compassion
Criticises	Wants harmony
Inauthentic	Authentic
Blames	Accepts flaws
Goal focused	Journey orientated

Ego vs higher self : examples of statements

Learn to recognise when you are acting from your ego and when you feel connected to your higher self. It is hard at first, but once you master it, the feeling of freedom and compassion is liberating.

Ego	Higher self
I never win anything.	I live a life of abundance; competition does not define me.
I need to always be perfect.	My imperfections contain wisdom and personality. I embrace who I am, creating space for others to feel safe & flawed too.
That person should be embarrassed laughing so loud.	How beautiful to see them lose themselves in the moment. Why might it bother me to see them having fun?
I'm not as good as that person.	I have my own charms; I respect that person's ability and drive.
I am the victim here.	I create my own reality; what lesson is to be learnt here?
Why's it raining today of all days, my coats not waterproof.	How lucky that I can head inside and dry off, and listen to the rain with a hot drink.
I need a new outfit to look my best at the dinner.	It's not my outfit that will make the dinner fun, it's the experience.

Spiritual health practices

You may gravitate towards holistic approach health treatments, there's so many with spiritual foundations, supported by science and proven results.

Therapies such as
Acupuncture
Ayurveda
Reiki
Sound healing
Yoga
Meditation
Breathwork
Theta healing
Hypnotherapy
Homeopathy

Kinesthetics, and many more, all fall under spiritual health treatments, that may boost your health, happiness, or wellness goals.

Your spiritual journey begins now.

Your spiritual journey may have already begun. A spiritual encounter may not be the psychedelic trip you were expecting; however, spiritual experiences vary greatly. Here's a small list of some you may have already witnessed.

- Overwhelming awe of nature, or sites on your travels.
- Questioning the deeper meaning.
- Seeking deeper connections.
- Expressing compassion for other beings.
- A sense that everything is as it should be.
- Noticing synchronicity.
- Feeling completely connected to your own body.
- A deep sense of inner peace.
- Exploring happiness beyond material possessions.

Spirituality and its mainline practices or ethics are becoming more prevalent in the modern world. It's becoming less of a word that drives a predisposition to show less respect to a spiritual person. It is no longer automatically perceived as woo woo, although there's still some work to be done, you may be surprised on your path or those around you on their own journey.

Your spiritual practice is personal, there's no cookie cutter one size fits all, it is what you want it to be, it's not linear, it's not a course with modules and exams that you must pass to move to the next activity or lesson. You can choose which practices you feel drawn or connected to, you do not have to be attracted to all of them. There are so many layers to spirituality, and it means something different for each individual. Please be kind to yourself as you approach this book, not everything will suit your journey. There may be additional practices that you will naturally seek out, there may be some that you dismiss at this stage. It's all cool. Take what you need. Revisit pages as often as you need. Read it methodically, or dip in and out of the chapters.

Earth grows
Fire glows
Air blows
Water flows
Soul knows

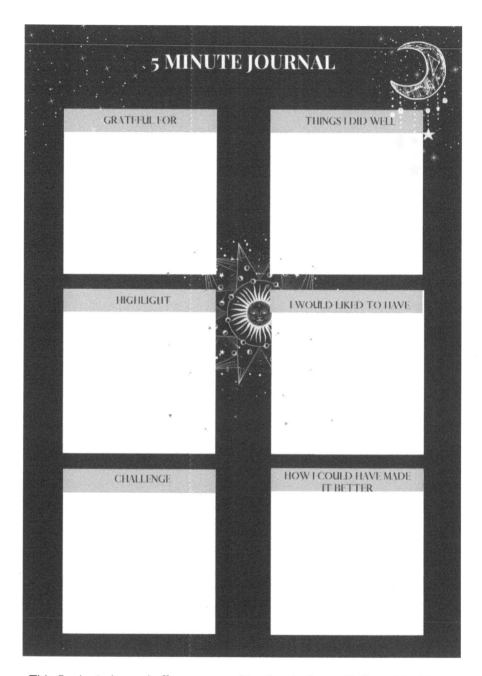

5 MINUTE JOURNAL

GRATEFUL FOR

THINGS I DID WELL

HIGHLIGHT

I WOULD LIKED TO HAVE

CHALLENGE

HOW I COULD HAVE MADE IT BETTER

This 5 minute journal offers some writing inspiration, with thoughts, ideas and reflective topics to jot down, throughout your inner glow journey.

Turning inwards

Inner Glow before you go.

For each statement, rate yourself out of 10, be honest, use the first number that comes to mind. Try not to be influenced by the score you would like, or the score you would like others to believe. Practise radical honesty with yourself. At the end of the book, you can revisit and update your scores.

0 is strongly disagree, 5 is neutral, 10 is strongly agree.

I understand spirituality
I have a spiritual practise
I feel grateful
I feel present
I feel aligned
I am happy
I am calm
I like my life
I have a purpose
I am in love with my life
I value experiences and connections
I feel connected to others
I feel connected to the world around me
I know how to manage my stress
I recognise where my life needs more attention/compassion
I feel connected to my body
I am in tune with my thoughts and emotions

I know how to relax my thoughts
I rarely feel stressed
I rarely feel anxious

Score /200

Affirmation for Joy

I take care of others when I fill my cup first.
Happiness and joy are to be experienced daily.
My life is wondrous and I take utter delight in my day.
I am loved and lovable.
I love freely.
My smile is contagious.
I am in love with my life.
This world is magical.
I see how I have been gifted.
I allow myself to be fully present.
It's ok to be silly.
My inner child has a voice.
I heal my body with laughter and play.
My soul shines brightly when I allow myself joy.

Intentions

What is an intention?

An intention is a way of being or feeling, it's how you want to show up to the world every day. Being clear on what you want from your life emotionally will help you to set intentions that connect with you. A clear intention that is attractive to your soul will in turn will help you to honour it. Provide yourself the opportunity to notice when you are taking actions or indulging in thoughts or activities that go against your intention.

Example – Your intention is to find joy in every day, yet you do not schedule any activities that make you smile, or book in any time with your sunshine crew, you sit down to watch a tearjerker film. It may not be self-sabotage, but your intention has no opportunity to manifest into reality. You are deserving of any intention you choose. It can be specific or a little ambiguous, as long as you know how you will feel when you honour your intention.

Example: Your intention is to find joy in every day. What does this intention mean to you? How will you know if you have honoured your intention? Is it if you smile or laugh more than you usually do? Does it mean to indulge in an unusual activity, or cutting out activities that do not bring you joy? How can you use your intention as a mantra throughout the day to keep you on track?

Why it is different to a goal.

Setting goals is future orientated and task focused, yet intentions are focused on keeping you grounded and present.

An intention is a way of being and how you want to feel. A goal or a resolution is something you want to accomplish.

Think about a goal you have – is the desired outcome something tangible, so that you feel good or accomplished?

What would happen if you set an intention focused on that emotion you desire instead?

Let's say your goal is to lose weight so that you feel more confident.

The goal is to lose weight, the desire (intention) is to feel more confident.

If you set your intention to, "I would like to feel more confident", you are casting a wider net, allowing yourself to be open to a multitude of ways to feel confident. You would explore ways daily to do so. Losing weight may be one of them, however you will be less attached to your weight daily, and more focused on how you always feel. Having this intention that requires you to investigate what it is that actually brings you confidence, rather than a narrow-minded view that losing weight will deliver you this feeling. Now, rather than worrying about daily weigh in's and all your hope and feelings of worth being attached to a number on the scale, you will find it easy to celebrate small wins and be kinder to yourself. There's no disappointment or defeat linked to the scales. In fact, there can't be any disappointment attached to your intention, as you are taking away the dread or possibility of failure. It all becomes a journey that is easy to reflect on and to pivot if the activities you choose are not linked to feeling confident. Feeling confident may not mean doing more and eating less, it may mean a social media diet to reduce opportunities of comparison, it can provide a deeper connection to your life as you get to ponder and articulate what exactly it is "feeling confident" looks like to you. Meals can still be enjoyable because they are not focused on being restrictive. There is no longer a maniacal attachment to weight.

Using an intention could mean that as part of your journey to feeling confident, you take up dance classes, to empower the way you move in your body, ahh what do you know, you ended up losing weight anyway, but it doesn't matter because you already learnt to love yourself and feel vibrant. You may even find confidence away from your target weight goal. Life is more enjoyable, because you are not obsessing over your diet or exercise, you understand that to enjoy life to the fullest, means being present and appreciating every day.

Goals are great, I am a huge fan. I invite you to explore an intention to assist, or replace your resolutions or goals, you will find a greater commitment, and sense of enjoyment on the journey. You may comprehend that your goal is completely unaligned with how you want to feel.

Goals with intentions

Try accompanying intentions to your goals, link an emotion or state of mind you desire, that is your driving force to the goals you have set yourself.

I want to lose 1kg to feel confident and be kinder to my body.

I want to get the promotion at work, so that I can feel proud of myself.

I want to get married, so that I can release the belief that I am unlovable.

The intention becomes your measure of success, rather than the "goal". Thus, improving daily happiness, as well as anchoring you to the present moment.

We often get caught up in milestones, I will be happier when I get the job, the car, the body. We forget what drives our desires. We want these things to feel a certain way. An intention is a way of being, a feeling, a state of mind you want to embrace into your daily life. Understanding your intention, allows you to live a life aligned with your values. Decisions will be made based on your energy, mental health and happiness, rather than material gains, statuses or titles.

It's about how you want to feel, not how society wants you to behave or achieve. We are raised with expectations, cultural pressures, and influences from family and society. We believe and place value on "what's expected of us". Intentions allow you to feel not only content and at peace with who you are as a person, but also to embrace and adore yourself and all your charms.

> *"Imagine if you made decisions based on how you would like to feel, or continue to feel, rather than what you believe is expected of you."*

The most common thing my clients and students tell me is they are happiest when creating, yet they have been raised by generations of doctors, grafters, and professionals and they were expected to follow suit, and on the way, they migrated away from creating. Another common theme is they would like to find more time for self-care yet run active households who place priority on always being busy. Intentions in these types of situations could be finding more time to indulge their creative side. Or an intention placed on inner peace or feeling less stressed. You know something must change, but without gaining clarity on what your internal needs and desires are, you cannot achieve them, and therefore cannot honour them, which in turn means anxiety rears its head, as you will naturally make decisions against your better judgement; restricting any possibility of an aligned life.

Think back to a time where you felt truly at peace, or blissfully happy. What were you doing? Were you deep in a hobby? Were you at work or travelling? Most likely you were enjoying the activity or stillness, without external influences, just your own choices to enjoy. Think of how amazing you felt that day. Imagine if you applied this theory *daily*.

How is it you really want to feel? Do you want to feel more or less of that emotion? How far removed are you from that reality?

If you want to feel inner peace, where are you currently? What is in your way, what distractions do you place in front of your peace?

What would have to happen throughout the day, for you to fall into bed peaceful and fulfilled?

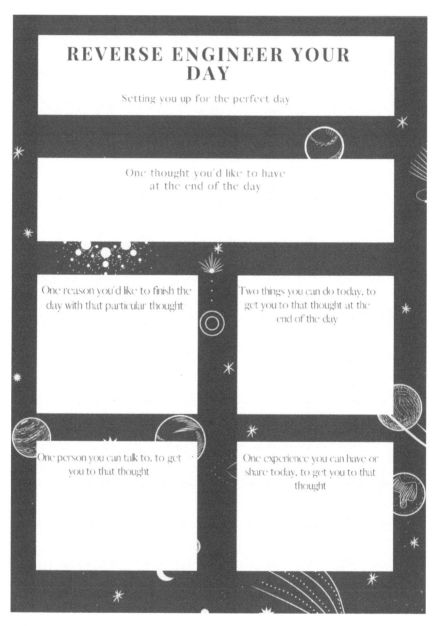

REVERSE ENGINEER YOUR DAY

Setting you up for the perfect day

One thought you'd like to have at the end of the day

One reason you'd like to finish the day with that particular thought

Two things you can do today, to get you to that thought at the end of the day

One person you can talk to, to get you to that thought

One experience you can have or share today, to get you to that thought

Use this reverse engineering your day worksheet, to help guide you to peaceful, fulfilled days.

5 reasons why intentions are important:

1. When you live aligned with your true needs, your anxiety reduces.

2. You know your worth and can recognise toxic relationships and activities easier. Self-sabotage becomes harder.

3. You will be less affected by the opinions of others or external comments, as you are unapologetically yourself and recognise the importance of honouring your intention.

4. It progressively becomes easier to set healthy boundaries, as you become aware of the damage to your way of being, and you have clarity of the negative impact of not setting.

5. Without understanding intention, you cannot acknowledge the needs that your soul requires you to meet for you to feel whole. The goal is almost empty, because you only know the shallow side of success, you will not be able to confirm if these goals are even yours or just an expectation you want to meet to please others.

Thoughts to explore, before setting an intention:

What matters most to me?
Where does my life feel unaligned?
What do I need to release or let go of?
What do I admire in others?
What do I struggle with?
Where could I use more happiness – in which areas of my life?

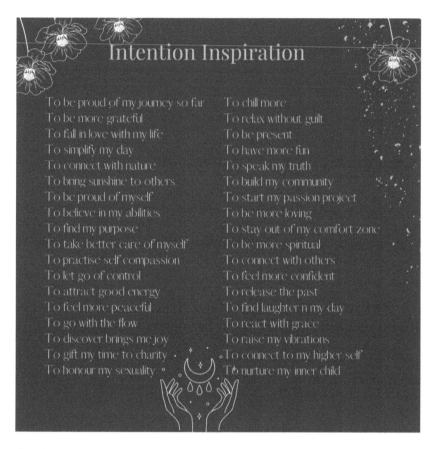

Intention Inspiration

To be proud of my journey so far
To be more grateful
To fall in love with my life
To simplify my day
To connect with nature
To bring sunshine to others
To be proud of myself
To believe in my abilities
To find my purpose
To take better care of myself
To practise self compassion
To let go of control
To attract good energy
To feel more peaceful
To go with the flow
To discover brings me joy
To gift my time to charity
To honour my sexuality

To chill more
To relax without guilt
To be present
To have more fun
To speak my truth
To build my community
To start my passion project
To be more loving
To stay out of my comfort zone
To be more spiritual
To connect with others
To feel more confident
To release the past
To find laughter in my day
To react with grace
To raise my vibrations
To connect to my higher self
To nurture my inner child

Self-discovery

Getting to know yourself. When was the last time you sat down and took inventory of your current situation, where you think you want to go, what you hope to do, or feel in this life? Taking time to turn inwards and reflect is fundamental to a meaningful life. We often believe we want certain things or experiences, yet we do not put the work in to achieve them. It is not laziness holding you back, it is potentially a lack of real desire, you simply want the things at surface level. Turning inwards will reveal your truest desires. Heads up – it may not be the thing you thought you most wanted or have been exerting the most effort to get. This is a beautiful 'getting to know you exercise', that you can repeat as often as you like. Naturally, your answers will morph throughout your life, or even in smaller periods of time. Really take the time to sit with your answers, being as honest as you can. These answers are solely for *you*. Try to write them as your truest self, without influence of what you think certain people in your life would like you to write, or what you think is expected of you.

Core Values

To live your most authentic, aligned life, it is essential to be acutely aware of your core values and beliefs, these are the attributes and traits you care about and stand for. These values help you know what is right and wrong for you, as well as influence how you interact with those around you. Your values highlight what is meaningful to you. You have most likely at one point been made aware of a company's core values, they utilise those values to make all decisions, and attract staff and customers who are aligned with those values. The values become the tone of voice for that company. Introducing, sharing, or learning about your own values can provide clarity to your journey, and highlight areas that need nurturing.

Examples of values – Joy, abundance, adventure, loyalty, wealth, development, challenge, compassion, responsibility, wisdom, commitment, bravery, determination, drive, play, cheerfulness, kindness, awareness, appreciation, diversity, community, integrity, honesty, truth, intimacy, respect, freedom, knowledge, equality, inclusion, recognition, security, family, friendship, relationships, structure, excitement, creativity.

Grab your journal and complete the exercise below, answering as honestly as possible.

What are my values? – Choose 3-5 that most resonate with you. Where do I live out of alignment with my values?

Do I have any conflict with any of my values?
Who most supports my values?
Who does not reflect my values?
How can I express these values more?

Mission statement

A mission statement is 1-2 sentences that summarises, what you stand for, what you are about, or here for, and if you are here to serve anyone or help a particular demographic. It brings purpose to your life. Often mission statements reflect your values. You most likely already have a mission statement at work, or for your business–this, however, is your personal one. This activity is great if you are feeling lost or at a crossroads. Once you have a mission statement, you can use it throughout the day as a mantra, you can use it as an affirmation for 'off' days, as well as for helping navigate decisions. Your mission statement is an anchor you can return to when you are feeling in a funk or disconnected. It is your life's purpose and becomes your legacy.

Before you start, explore the below questions, and revisit your value answers.

What do I want to be known for?
How do I want to impact others?
How would I like to be remembered?
What impact do I want to make in this life?
Why is that impact important to me?
What do I stand for?
Am I here to serve/help others? If so, who?
What's my purpose?
When did I last have a purpose?
Are there injustices I would really like to tackle? (It is more than ok for this to not form your mission statement; your statement doesn't have to be world domination level)

With your mission statement, think about your ultimate life

goal, your characteristics, and the way in which you want to achieve this.

Example.

Goal – To raise a family. To bring happiness to others. To eradicate the gender pay gap. To educate. To be famous.

Characteristics – Funny, compassionate, serious, courageous, kind, knowledgeable, efficient.

Impact – Playful, informative, inclusive, nurturing, disruptive, professionally, holistically, globally, continuingly, help others, share.

Mission statement drawn from the above would be – "I strive to be a teacher that students gravitate towards, I will do this, by delivering playful adventurous life lessons in a nurturing environment.

If you are unsure of your ultimate life goal, then reverse it – choose your impact, then your characteristics to produce your why.

Impact – I want to have a global impact.

Values – I am playful and kind.

Goal announces itself – I will do this by...

My mission statement is...

Soul alignment

To further understand your purpose and soul desires, think about the questions below, documenting both your thoughts and actions in your journal.

Career

Is having a career important to me?
Am I finding or creating my dream job?
What am I most afraid of in my work life?
Who is a person I admire in their work life?
What about this person do I admire?
What do they do differently?
Could I learn something from them?

If money were no object, what job would I do?
Is my work-life balance healthy?
Do I feel respected at work?
Do I feel fairly remunerated for my work?

Love
What are my favourite memories?
Where do I struggle to show vulnerability?
Are there ways I struggle to display love and affection?
When do I feel happiest?
What behaviours do I admire in others?
What am I most afraid of?
What do I need to let go of?
Do I receive the intimacy I crave?

Soul
What's the most beautiful thing about my life?
What is my soul purpose?
How can I simplify life?
How can I speak kinder to myself?
What am I curious about?
What guilt do I hold on to?

Life
What stresses me?
What, or who, do I struggle to say no to?
Where do I struggle to be assertive?
What are my barriers?
What must change?
What drains me?
How am I privileged?
What do I take for granted?
Who am I performing for?
Where can I show more discipline?
What takes a lot of my attention?
What am I in control of?
What would I like to be in control of?

Inner Peace

I feel most peaceful when…
When did I last feel peaceful?
I feel least at peace when…
How can I improve my self-care?
How can I show more love and compassion for others?
What do I strongly dislike doing?

Play

20 things that bring me joy are…
How often do I make time for these joyful things?
How can I loosen up more?
What holds me back from having fun?
What happens when I restrict my play?

Passion

What sets my heart on fire?
What do I love about my life?
What things motivate me?
Have I suppressed any passions of mine?
What topics do I feel passionate about?

Health

What are my mental unhealthy habits?
What are my physical unhealthy habits?
How can I reduce toxic activities?
What soothes me when I feel anxious?
What are my negative habits?
How can I be kinder to myself?
What are my health goals?

Self-view

What do I love about myself? Try to list 10 things.
I am worth knowing because...
How do I leave others feeling?
How would I like to leave others feeling?
What are my charms?

What holds me back?
What's missing from my life?
What emotion would I like more of?
What emotion would I like less of?
How would I like to feel more confident?
What is the worst thing you can say about me?
What behaviours do I dislike in others?

5 years future me
Think ahead 5 years, complete this exercise as if money was no issue.
What do you spend your time doing?
Where do you live?
How do you want to spend your days?
How many hours a day/week do you work, if any?
What are you wearing?
Who are you with?
How do you feel when you wake up?
What are your hobbies?
How much are you earning?
What's in your savings account?
What plans are in your diary?
How do you feel when you go to bed?

Limitless me
What would I do if money were no object?
What would I do if people wouldn't judge me?
What would I do if I knew I couldn't fail?
What one thing would improve my life?
How would my life be improved?
What opinions am I afraid of others holding about me?
What stops me from having inner peace?
What limiting beliefs hold me back from a sense of peace?
How can I care for myself more?
How can I create time in my schedule to find and explore inner peace?

What would I love to achieve this year?
What activities/experiences have I always wanted to try?

Goals

List 50 things you would like to do in this lifetime.

Rank each answer out of 10 based on how much you would like to do it.

Now next to that list, add a timeframe when you would like to do it by. Use 6 months, 1 year, 2 years, 5 years, 10 years and above 10 years.

Journal any unexpected goals or time frames from your list. Why do they feel unexpected?

Activity – What takes my time?

Create a schedule, either paper or digital, and allocate specific colours for the following activities – work, hobbies, down time, commuting, chores, family, friends, exercise, sleep, and relationship time. You can swap or add any additional relevant activities but try not to subcategorize too much as it can make it harder to analyse. At the end of each day, or throughout the day, allocate relevant colours to every hour. At the end of the week, take time to reflect on how your time is spent and any changes you would like to see. What is the optimum ratio for each colour?

Affirmation for Creativity

I express myself creatively.
I speak my truth through my creations.
My inner child loves my creative way.
The world takes joy in my creativity.
There is beauty in my creations.
I am allowed to express myself.
I embrace my sexuality.
Each of my creations tells a story.

Meditation and Mindfulness

Meditation is a mind and body practice to train attention and awareness and to reduce racing thoughts and attachment to emotions. Meditation comes in various forms of teachable techniques that can be built on in the same way you would learn anything new.

Mindfulness is the act of being present, being aware, and observing thoughts and emotions without judging or analysing them.

It has been many years now since the opinion that meditation is for monks. These days it's common for top CEOs, professional athletes & Olympians, creators, and artists, as well as people you may know personally, to speak of their own personal meditation practice and the benefits. We are now in an age where meditation is welcomed and recommended by an array of wellness leaders and scientists. Every practitioner will speak of their own personal experiences of meditation and the benefits of a regular practice. Below, we have listed proven benefits to individuals from regular meditation practice.

Benefits of meditation:

- Improved sleep.
- Reduced stress and anxiety.
- Higher sense of enjoyment in daily activities.
- Improved gratitude and a greater sense of contentment.
- Increased attention span.

- Proven to help overcome addictions.
- Linked to lessen pain.
- Increased density of grey matter in the brain – allowing for deeper self-awareness and empathy.
- Ability to be truly present.
- Able to witness thoughts and emotions, without guilt, judgement, or attachment to outcome.
- Reduced activity in the Posterior cingulate – (PCC) the "me" part of the brain, linked to wandering mind and daydreaming. Minds that wander are less likely to feel happy and content and are inclined to worry about the past and future, rather than be present.
- Temporoparietal junction – (TPJ) becomes active. This part of the brain is responsible for empathy, sense of compassion and perspective.
- Amygdala – this part of the brain is responsible for feelings of anxiety fear and stress, this thankfully shrinks during meditation.
- Reduces activity in the default mode network (DMN) – DMN is our inner voice – the monkey mind, that constant chatter.
- Generates high levels of kindness and compassion, for yourself and for others.
- Higher levels of empathy – which in turn provides greater peace as your perspective has shifted.
- Greater self-awareness – Self-awareness allows us to see events more factually, instead of from your emotional point of view, thus allowing you to step back and see the whole picture, rather than being caught up in how it made you feel. It also helps you grow and cultivate stronger relationships.
- Inner peace – that beautiful blissful state.

Why should I meditate and practice mindfulness?

The world we inhabit is full of stimulants and stressors.

The modern world is full of: chores, activities, recommendations, expectations, self-help images that show you are not good enough, people and dependants relying on you, family members guilting you, traffic causing your already tight schedule to run over into your already limited free time, car troubles, long crowded public journeys, junk food diets, lack of sleep, unrealistic workloads, bright artificial lights, a lack of green areas, and a constant attachment to electronic devices.

All these stimulants and stressors add up, even when we do not realise, we are over stimulated. Everyone feels these often-invisible struggles, the brain is too noisy, you become unable to switch off, you receive no break from the constant chatter of your own thoughts and to do lists. It becomes harder to find clarity on situations and decisions, racing thoughts blur into a jumbled mess, and it is impossible to filter out the noise or step back to see the bigger picture. Think of a snow globe, shaken into oblivion – you cannot see the image. You instead focus on the snow dancing around. The snow globe is your mind, the snow represents your thoughts, constantly chasing one thought, to the next, there is no opportunity to enjoy the view, as here the snow never settles. The snow globe is continually disrupted. You accept that, this is how life is, constantly hectic and noisy, even in silence. You know there's a pretty view behind the chatter or flurry of snow. You will get to see it one day. Introducing meditation and mindfulness to your life, allows the snow to settle in the snow globe. Your thoughts slow down, gifting you with clarity and much needed headspace.

Much like muddy water – you cannot see to the bottom. There is an ancient story of a princess who drops her crown into the water, pure panic follows as the whole village – desperate to help – jump into the water. Many lay on the bank of water and reach in with their arms to try and find the crown for the distraught princess. The more activity that happened in the water, the muddier it got. Soon you could no longer even see the shimmer of the crown. A wise villager asked everyone to get out of the water, for he had a plan. Begrudgingly they all agreed, the wise villager then simply sat by the bank. Outraged everyone started raising voices, how dare this person risk the crown being lost forever!? How can they sit there and do nothing?! The wise villager simply accepted the concerns, and still he stayed motionless. Time started to pass, the princess was still distraught, and the angry villagers had started to noisily whisper about this silly tactic, of course no one noticed that the water had once more become still, that the mud had started to settle and once more you could see the bottom. The wise villager simply waited for the muddy water to settle, so that he could dip his arm in and pick up the crown that was revealed, glimmering at the bottom.

Our minds are the muddy water, we try to calm our over-active thoughts or find results, by adding more activities, more questions and thoughts; when the biggest relief we can offer ourselves is to step back and take a moment. To allow our answers to reveal themselves. When highly effective CEO's, inventors and creators are interviewed and asked about how they came up with their greatest ideas, no one ever says in the boardroom, or in a meeting. It's often in a dream, at the gym, whilst creating, or whilst relaxing. It's in an altered state of mind – that 'flow' state or in an environment of calm.

Stress, anxiety, and overstimulated minds, have physical manifestations in the body – tight muscles, tension headaches, grinding teeth, poor skin, limited sleep, frown lines, poor digestion, some illness and skin conditions may flare up. Internally, relationships suffer, work becomes harder, you may not find any joy in the day, you become exhausted and cancel events and activities that usually promote your health and wellbeing. You then turn towards more stimulants, it's a never-ending cycle. You can't switch off, you get no rest, you lay in bed mind racing, unable to name the root cause of your anxiety or heightened state of awareness. The next day brings you more of the same.

Mindfulness and meditation provide respite from these undesirable states and over time reduce physical symptoms. When the noise quiets, you see clearer, allowing time to reflect and learn about yourself. Improving self-worth and compassion, which in turn, leads to greater tolerance of the world around you.

These practices improve your physical wellbeing and circulation. They reduce the risk of migraines and headaches, lower heart problems and aid high blood pressure ailments, and are even known to help battle addictions and overcome desires.

Ponder a time or event that caused you upset or annoyance, an occasion you have spent hours or days revisiting. Everyone has at least one situation that really riled them up. A situation that you have replayed repeatedly in your head, losing so much precious time, you probably even recruited people to join in those emotions with you, sharing your perspective with friends so they validate your sense of injustice. Thinking back on this event, it may even respark those feelings or annoyance or anger.

What benefits has living in this memory had for you? What problems have you been able to solve, by letting this irritating situation live rent free in your head?

Imagine if you settled the mind instead, providing yourself some closure by stepping back and observing the situation without an emotional perspective. As you observe this memory, try to view it as an outsider without any attachment to an outcome, and without a bias of any other people involved. Witness the memory objectively as you notice thoughts and allow them to pass. Try not to judge either party involved. Are you noticing any differences to the situation this time? Has it re-sparked the same initial anger or annoyance?

I had a fantastic mentor, early in my career, I remember calling her to moan about a situation. I was leading a project and not getting the response I needed from my peers. I was so annoyed about it. Michelle listened to me rant about my frustrations and the impact these people were having on my day. Her response was, "Gem, when you are feeling annoyed because someone has pissed you off, you gotta ask yourself, did they piss you off on purpose? If you believe that they did, then sure, be mad, and address it respectfully, but if you step back and see that they didn't purposely set out to upset or anger you, then why are you mad? Learn to appreciate their priorities don't have to match yours, which means their values and beliefs are different too. It doesn't make them bad, so don't hold it in your heart. Let it go, learn what you can do to infl uence in positive ways that don't bring a dark cloud over your day." I cannot tell you how many times I have applied this theory since, each time reminds me of the power of non-attachment.

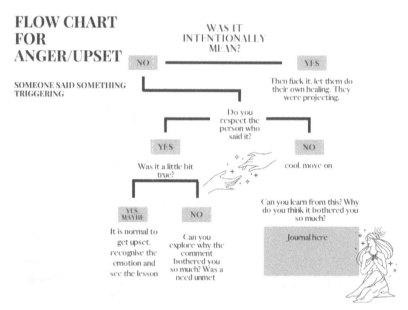

FLOW CHART FOR ANGER/UPSET

SOMEONE SAID SOMETHING TRIGGERING

WAS IT INTENTIONALLY MEAN?

NO — YES

Then fuck it, let them do their own healing. They were projecting.

Do you respect the person who said it?

YES — NO

cool, move on

Was it a little bit true?

Can you learn from this? Why do you think it bothered you so much?

YES, MAYBE — NO

It is normal to get upset, recognise the emotion and see the lesson

Can you explore why the comment bothered you so much? Was a need unmet

Journal here

I even made a handy flow chart, for you to check in with yourself, when you feel triggered, or upset by a comment or incident.

Attachment vs nonattachment?

Buddha teaches us that the root of all suffering is attachment.

So, we practice non-attachment – the art of letting go of thoughts and emotions that create suffering.

Think of attachment as you would expectations – expectations for life itself, or for events or individuals. How many times have you daydreamed of an event, in your head creating details, conversations, emotions, desired outcomes, even relationship statuses, only to find the event completely anticlimactic? The event simply could not live up to your expectations. You were so attached to your desired outcome, that you couldn't fully enjoy the gift of the event, not to men-tion the lost hours you spent daydreaming rather than being present. Compare that to the random nights out you have had, the short notice ones, completely unplanned. No time to spend hours mentally visualising the perfect outfit, no predisposed ideas of who you will see or meet. You haven't created an ideal framework in your head, so everything that happens is simply joyous and fantastic.

For some, there's an expectation for what life will be, what they believe it should be, and there's no room to pivot or change direction, even if they are not experiencing happiness. We all have our own expectations we need to explore, in order to practice non-attachment, so that we can fully experience life.

I was talking to a student this morning. Recently, along with his friend and business partner, he had started investing in stocks and shares. Last night saw a turn for one of their shares, their first investment of which they all brought large amounts, was already up 300%. The market analysts are saying it hasn't hit its peak and forecast another huge growth by the end of the year, which could mean extreme financial gain for them all. Life changing amounts. Naturally, they were all on their group chat discussing what they would buy, how amazing life will be, the usual "if I won the lottery" conversation. Man, I was so proud of my student, he turned around to his mate, who had just wished to fast forward the next 6 months so they could find out the final fate, and he said, "ok it's cool when it happens, but you can't start wishing away life now, life is the next 6 months. You get that money, and you might get a bigger house, a newer car, but your life is the same, you still gotta take your little one to the same school gates every morning, you're not gonna change schools and take her away from her friends, you're still married to the same woman, you just take more holidays and worry about bills less. Don't go wishing away the next 6 months when you are already experiencing life, you got to enjoy what you have now, or this money won't bring you the happiness you think it will."

That my beauties is non-attachment. It will be cool if that happens, but I am cool if it doesn't. Meditation and mindfulness will get you there.

"It is what it is."

Non-attachment can also be described as non-acceptance.

An example of non-acceptance would be hitting traffic, non-accepting thoughts would be, "Urgh there's traffic, this always happens to me! I didn't want traffic today, this is just my luck. I don't like sitting in traffic."

An accepting thought would be, "oh, traffic."

Brain wave states and how they change during mindfulness and meditation.

Our brain frequencies change throughout the day, it's no surprise that we do not operate at one flat level. Activities and other factors can influence our brain frequency.

Gamma state – 30-100hz Awareness. State of hyperactivity. This is the best time to learn and to listen. Although gamma can sometimes be a bit "can't see the woods for the trees."

Beta state – 13-30hz Alertness. Most common – this is your thinking/working mind. This state is for processing and planning, it's analytical. This is linked to your prefrontal cortex which is important for decision making.

Alpha state – 9-13hz Relaxed. Brain waves start to calm down, migrating away from the thinking brain. Neutral integration means both hemispheres are in balance. You may notice this state after a walk in nature or a relaxing activity. You are lucid and reflective here, creating the perfect opportunity to take information into the subconscious.

Theta state – 4-8hz Deeply relaxed. Sometimes known as flow state. This is where the verbal thinking mind transitions to the meditative/visual mind. We move from the planning mind into a deeper state of awareness. Theta is associated with visualisations, we develop a stronger intuition, more capacity for oneness, wholeness, and connection. Here we are capable of solving complex problems. This is particularly useful in sports, as the analytical judgmental brain has been overridden by the subconscious. Therefore, the mind body connection is optimized, removing the ego from the game.

Delta state – 1-3hz. Sleeping. Although, after years of dedicated practice, some can reach this state in an awakened state, for most of us, we simply reach this state during a deep, dreamless sleep.

During meditation, the frontal cortex switches off, that's the overactive thinking/planning/analysing part of the brain. How amazing would it be to be able to switch that off and get respite from the thousand thoughts running through your head every minute?

History of meditation

Meditation is one of the oldest activities, and it really has stood the test of time. From early cave drawings to integration into therapy and schools.

A BRIEF HISTORY OF
MEDITATION

Meditation is a techinque to train the mind to be present and aware.

A BRIEF HISTORY OF
MEDITATION

Modern day meditation in the Western world

5000 BC

Wall art in caves in India ,images of men seated with eyes half closed

1500 BC

Written evidence of meditation is revealed in the Vedas, ancient Hindu texts.

1958

Jack Kerouac releases Dharma bums, a book following 2 young men, on their journey for truth. Adventure in the pursuit of the Zen way.

1970'S

The Vipassana movement starts in the US

5TH-6TH CENTURY

Bodhidharma, a prince born in South India, travels to China to share his learnings, becoming the founder of Zen Buddhism

5TH-6TH CENTURY

Siddhartha Gautama, later known as Buddha, was a religious and spiritual teacher and philosopher in Ancient India, believed to be the founder of Buddhism

1960'S

Maharishi Manesh becomes the founder of Transcendental meditation

6TH-4TH BCE CENTURY

Taoist(also spelt Daoist) meditation starts to develop their own techniques, however it is argued that evidence for meditation in China, dates back to the 3rd and 4th century

1960'S

Yoga and meditation becomes popular in the US and Europe

7TH CENTURY

In 653 the first meditation hall is opened, in Japan

1970'S

Clinical scientific studies of meditation begin.

10TH-14TH CENTURY

Meditation is adopted in many religions including Christianity, Judaism and Sufism- a form of Islam

8TH CENTURY

Zen Buddhism spreads across Korea, China, Vietnam & Japan

1970'S

Jon Kabat Zin opens the centre for mindfulness, teaching Mindfulness-Based Stress Reduction (MBSR)

18TH CENTURY

Schopenhauer a German philosopher showed a keen interest in meditation, he both studied and admired meditation.

1990'S

Deepak Chopra meditation centre opens.

2014

Deepak Chopra hosts the worlds largest meditation, 33061 people attend online

1922

Herman Hesse releases a book on meditation, called Siddharta

2017

US military hosts meditation training for Veterans as alternative therapy for PTSD

1927

"Bardol Thodol" a spiritual book on Buddhism, known in the West as "Tibetan book of death" Instructing the art of dying. This book references meditation heavily.

2007

Meditation is introduced to schools in the states, including Visitacion valley middle school in San Francisco.

2019

U.K schools start teaching mindfulness and meditation as part of the curriculum. Both primary and secondary schools.

Types of meditation

Mindfulness meditation
Involves focusing on one activity. Stay focused on what you're doing, allowing yourself to be present in the moment, noticing every detail of the task at hand. Practicing non-judgemental compassion, staying curious. A more detailed example follows later in this chapter.

Loving kindness meditation
Turn your attention inwards and imagine joy swirling in your heart, allow feelings of love and warmth to build in your chest.

Now choose an affirmation or wish, for example, "May I be happy and free."

Then direct that statement to someone you love. "May (insert loved one's name) be happy and free."

Now someone you feel neutral towards, maybe a colleague or neighbour. "May (insert neutral acquaintance name) be happy and free."

Next is someone you dislike or are having a challenging time with. "May (challenging person's name) be happy and free."

Think about all these people together as a group and send them the same message, "May they all be happy and free."

Finish imaging all the people in the world, direct the same love note to all the beings on the planet. "May (everyone on the planet) be happy and free."

Transcendental meditation
During this meditation, a silent mantra is repeated. You can choose a mantra that is close to your heart, an affirmation, or you may choose a mantra in your mother tongue or an ancient language such as Sanskrit. The mantra is your anchor to keep your mind from wandering. Some people use mala beads. Each bead is passed through the fingers in count with a repeated manta. Most mala beads have 108

beads and a larger guru bead, so that you can recognise one round. 108 is a spiritual significant number.108 is special in maths, spirituality, and the universe. The mathematical significance is in the elegance of its geometry. In maths, 108 is referred to as a "natural number" for how it is found on Earth, as well as the planets and the galaxy. Universally speaking the diameter of the sun is 108 times that of the earth. The distance between the sun and earth is 108 times the diameter of the sun. The distance between earth and the moon is 108 times the diameter of the moon. There are 108 spiritual places in India. 108 sacred spots/pressure points in the body, as well as 108 energy lines, known as Nadi's in the body.

1 is the absolute 0 is the cosmos and 8 is infinite.

Zen Meditation

Here posture is especially important, it focuses heavily on Zazen, "the sitting", releasing attachment whilst suspending all thoughts and judgements. You may hear it referred to as "zazen plus zero" meaning sitting plus nothing. In Zen meditation the goal is to separate from the ego.

Traditionally you sit on a zafu, a special meditation cushion, in a lotus position (*Kekkafuza* in Japanese), or half lotus (*Hankafuza* in Japanese). The cushion elevates the hips allowing the knees to lower to the ground, you may additionally have a zabuton which is a larger cushion to go under the zafu, softening the knees. If flexibility – as it is for most of us – does not allow for lotus or half lotus, you can choose seiza which is kneeling, with the bum resting on the heels. Or a gentler variation is a meditation stool or chair. In Zazen the teeth are together, and your tongue stays at the roof of your mouth, eyes are open, resting on the floor about a metre in front of you. It is recommended to sit facing a wall to avoid distractions.

Hands are in the cosmic mudra – *hokkajin* in Japanese, left hand sits on the right palms facing the sky, tips of the thumbs touch, hands rest in the lap.

Breathing is done through the nose, both inhaling and exhaling. There is less focus on the breath in Zazen meditation, let long breaths be long and short breaths be short.

*Before investing in a zafu – try folding some blankets to sit on creating height, to explore this posture.

Spiritual meditation

This is a way to link to your higher being and connect with spirit guides and ancestors. Many styles fall under this category, including kundalini and specific guided meditations. For spiritual meditation explore thoughts of being conscious and aware before starting the chosen mediation style.

Kundalini meditation

Kundalini teachings were first noted in ancient Hindu religious texts called the Upanishads. Kundalini was a very private practice, with only established students, who had dedicated years to spirituality, invited to learn. Over the years the teachings have become popular after being introduced to the west in the 1960's by yogi Bhajan. Kundalini belief is that energy lays at our root chakra – the base of the spine, coiled like a snake. To awaken this energy, allows kundalini to rise through the centre of the body, unblocking all 7 chakras, making its way to the crown and out of the body, reaching a great spiritual awakening and bliss. Many practitioners choose to wear light clothing – or white outfits – and cover their heads with white fabrics or shawls to promote energy flow. The meditation begins in the same posture options, and a focus on the breath to stay in the meditative state. Activating the third eye can be achieved by looking at the space between the eyebrows, with closed eyes. Many mudras hand gestures are used, as well as chants and external or internal mantras. Sohum is a common mantra. Sohum means, *"I am that"*. To really utilise the mantra, you connect it to the breath. On the inhale "So" and "hum" on the exhale. Kundalini spiritual awakening symptoms include seeing vivid colours, tingling sensations in arms and legs, intense heat in the spine, and feelings of ecstasy or bliss.

Vipassana meditation

This is insight meditation, self-observing (Buddhist). During this, you work on turning inwards and simplifying the language. Special seeing, to deepen awareness of the body. Interruptions are ok to become aware of, if you hear a loud noise of a door closing then you acknowledge by internally saying "hearing, hearing", or if you witnessed a visual interruption, you would internally say "seeing, seeing". Notice sensations as soft or warming rather than physical objects. Mental objects, thoughts or visuals are acknowledged as "thinking", "remembering", "imagining", and "creating".

As you close practice you continue with the gradual coming back by thinking to yourself "opening, opening" as you open your eyes, "returning returning" as you come back to the room and physical environment.

Group meditation

This can be a great experience, as all practitioners in the

room, or space, are all directing positive energy to the same place. It's not uncommon for the whole group to hold hands or discuss the meditation subject before the start. This is often a guided meditation, hosted by a meditation teacher. Afterwards there are often herbal teas and a chance to share experiences if you wish.

Moving meditation

Mostly in the style of dance or yoga. People often talk about that "flow state" when you are in the zone — time has no concept, and you are fully absorbed in the activity. Many people find this in their love or passion – maybe art or music. It is also possible to find in movement. This may be when you are letting go and feeling free enough to move your body intuitively without fear or restrictions. It may also be in a repeated movement. In yoga, to celebrate certain occasions, such as change of seasons, yogis will do 108 sun salutations. It is reported that yogis find a beautiful flow state where the body glides through these movements, almost on muscle memory; finding a meditative state.

Tai chi Taoist meditation

Dated back to 1670, although tai chi was designed for self-defence it is also focused on finding serenity in gentle flowing movements.

Qigong

Dated back 4000 years, Qigong is often mistaken with tai chi, both practices are focused on moving chi. Chi translates as "vital energy" known in yoga as prana. In Qigong standing movements are linked with breath – to master your energy, promoting calm.

Visual meditation also known as gazing meditation or trataka.

You choose an object, a flame, or a photo, most objects are symbolic to the practitioner. You sit with the flame or object at eye level. This meditation works by staring at the flame and not moving – your mind will not send any new visual information to the brain, slowly your peripheral vision will fade out, heightening your awareness of the flame, until it is all that you see. Ultimately becoming one with the candle. You may notice tears forming, it is believed this is cleansing. Contradictions – be mindful if you have sight issues or suffer migraines. The object does not have to be a flame, do not overstress the eyes.

Yoga nidra

Yoga nidra is also known as yogic sleep. It is typically practiced for 30/40 minutes as a guided meditation, for which you will be laid on the floor. Yoga nidra works through five koshas, or sheaths. These five koshas cover the atman – atman being the Sanskrit word for 'soul'.

The koshas are annamayya, pranamaya, manomaya, vijnanamaya, and anadamaya. (Physical body, energy body, emotional body, wisdom body, and bliss body.)

Your teacher will guide you through these layers, think of it as Russian dolls – one must be opened to reach the next. During yoga nidra you reach a deep state of relaxation, finding a state between waking and sleeping. A 30-minute yoga nidra can have more benefit than 3 hours of sleep.

Myths about meditation

There are so many misconceptions about meditation. I am here to tell you – you can do it on your own terms, for as long or as short a practice as you need.

When I was first offered meditation, my beliefs were:

You have to close your eyes. *Well, this made me feel vulnerable.*

You have to be seated. *It's not comfortable to sit cross-legged for most of us.*

You have to do it in silence. *Urgh, back then, silence was my nemesis.*

You have to be still. *Yeah, that's not going to work for me, it's hard to sit still.*

You have to chant. *Weird, again, this made me feel vulnerable.*

You need to shave your head, vow silence and wear orange. *Nope.*

You have to do it for hours/days at a time. *Too busy babe.*

That it's religious. *I am not religious.*

It felt overwhelming. Unaligned with my energy and lack of religious beliefs, I was far too busy to sit still and do nothing for an hour. The idea of a silent day was utterly horrifying. Thankfully, I no longer feel that way and have embraced a regular meditation practice that suits my lifestyle.

So, to reconfirm you don't have to shave your head and do a 6-month monastery retreat.

You can be comfy, you can be still, you can also find a meditative state in movement.

You can have music in the background, you may even find the flow state by singing yourself.

You can do it in silence, or with the regular noise of your home around you.

You can stand, lay down, walk, or move mindfully.

You can be silent if you want to, or you may choose to repeat an affirmation or mantra out loud.

Chanting's cool if you like it, it's never necessary. I quite like it now, but it's been a journey.

You can do 3-minute meditations, 5 minutes or 1 hour. No one is timing you.

You can do shower meditations.

You can always expand the length of time as you get more comfortable and familiar. It's your practice. I recommend you start with a short daily practice. Be kind to yourself if you miss a day and start again. If it feels too much still, just start in a comfy position with a short, guided meditation with a topic you are drawn to.

Tips before you start.

How – Find your most comfortable seated position, this may be on a chair. Perhaps you sit on the floor with or without a cushion. Legs can be crossed naturally; you may choose lotus or half lotus depending on flexibility. Another option is to kneel with the glutes on the ankle.

Location – Somewhere you can relax uninterrupted, this can be indoors or outside, try not to be too cold or too warm.

Time – The time that is best for you, some practitioners recommend as soon as you wake. I am a big fan of not forcing a schedule to your meditation, although you may find it easier to form a habit this way. If you are very tight for time you may introduce a guided yoga nidra to your day as you fall asleep.

Noises – You can choose to meditate in quiet, to music, or to a guided meditation.

Mantra or chant – A mantra is a sound or phrase that you can use to deepen your meditation, you may choose to repeat it internally, or chant out loud. You do not have to do either.

Object to look at – If you are doing a fixed gaze meditation you may want a lit candle or an object to gaze at.

To get started

Explore thoughts and ideas that you know may pop up during your practice, see if you can come to peace with these thoughts before you start. Over time, during your meditation you will be able to witness these thoughts without attachment.

Let's do a seven-point posture check.

Sitting – Allow the body to find comfort in the seated position of your choice.

Spine – To avoid back pain, ensure your spine is as straight as possible, if you have rounded shoulders or your spine sinks when you sit, roll up a towel or small blanket into a wedge shape, and pop it under the back of the glutes, this will help open your chest. Alternatively sit against a wall.

Hands – You may choose a mudra. Gyan mudra is a popular one that improves concentration, your index finger meets the thumb — imagine the OK hand gesture, you then face the palm upwards, the back of the hands rests on the knees. Hands can also rest on your knees palms down. You may choose to cup the hands in the centre of your lap. If you cup hands, rest your non-dominant on top, to suppress and submit the dominant hand.

Shoulders – Shoulders should be pulled down and away from the ears, opening your heart and chest.

Chin – To reduce neck pain you may choose to slightly lift or lower the chin, to lengthen the spine, relax the muscles of the face.

Jaw – Create some space between the teeth to allow the jaw to relax, you may wish to exaggerate a yawn a few times to stretch the jaw in preparation.

Eyes – Most people choose to close the eyes completely in a resting state, alternatively, you may wish to soften your gaze, lower your eyes slightly and keep an unfocused gaze on the floor in front of you. Try to commit to open or closed eyes before you start, so as not to disrupt your meditation.

You are now ready to begin your meditation, it's normal for the monkey mind to be active, everyone has thoughts at the start of their practice often "I wonder if I am doing this right", and "I shouldn't have any thoughts at all". Be kind to yourself, you will experience thoughts, this is not you doing it wrong, it is simply the overactive state of mind, and with time—as with everything in life—it gets easier. Try to observe emotions without absorbing them. As a thought arises, witness it as a stranger, observe the thought or emotion without judgement or analysing, simply become aware of the thought, and allow it to move on. If you are struggling to allow these emotions to pass, bring your focus to your breath, notice every detail of the breath, where the breath starts low in your belly or chest, how it moves through your body like waves. Allow yourself to relax with every exhale, become so focused on the breath, that maybe you even feel the breeze on the space below your nose, or the change in temperature as you breathe out.

As your mind wanders, return your focus to your breath. This will happen many times.

As you come to the end of your meditation, return to your body slowly, try to avoid rushing back to the hectic world. This time is for you. Take a moment to slowly open the eyes, to explore, and to notice how you are feeling and any sensations as they arise.

Breathwork for meditation

Pranayama is known in Sanskrit as 'life force', it's the oxygen we need to exist. By manipulating the breath in the body, we can change our energy, and calm our mind, amongst many other wonderful things. Breathwork is a fantastic anchor to the present moment and a destroyer of anxiety. There are so many examples of pranayama for you to explore. I have included a few here that you can use as part of your mediation practice, as well as stand-alone activities.

Belly breathing

Breathing through the nostrils, rather than the mouth, take the deepest inhale that you have taken all day, and exhale slowly. Notice how your body moved with the deep inhale, as you filled your chest with air, your shoulders moved up towards your ears, and your rib cage expanded.

This time, instead of sending the breath into the chest, can you breathe into your belly? As women we spend most of our adult life sucking the belly in. Throw off the shackles and get comfy. Allow the belly to inflate, as if you are blowing up a balloon. Inhaling, the belly rises, on the exhale the belly falls back down. Try a few more times, inhale, the belly rises, exhale, the belly falls.

Notice how the body responds to belly breathing, you may feel the body soften, and relax, as the inhales become enjoyable, and the mind slows down. When you first start belly breathing, it may be a challenge that you may need to actively remind yourself of, avoid drawing the navel in on the inhales.

Belly breathing will forever be one of my favourite breaths, I do it frequently throughout my day as I find it wonderfully peaceful. I highly recommend it during moments of stress or anxiety, as you can do it unnoticed. Simply send the breath into the belly, rather than the chest.

Alternate nostril breathing

Sitting comfortably with a straight spine. Eyes can be open or closed throughout.

Place your right thumb on your right nostril, peace fingers on the space between your eyebrows – your third eye. Inhale deeply and with slow control through your left nostril. Now close your left nostril with your ring finger and little finger, as you lift your thumb off the right nostril. Exhale through the right nostril with slow control. Next Inhale is through the right nostril, close the right nostril with the thumb again, as you open the left nostril to exhale, next inhale is through the left nostril, exhaling through the right. Do this for a couple of minutes, keeping the shoulders relaxed. This is a beautiful way to prepare yourself for meditation. Simply drop your hands into your lap and begin your meditation when you are ready.

Breath retention

There are many many variations of breath retention, and

a multitude of benefits. If you are new to breath retention, I recommend the usual seated position. Inhale slowly through the nose, hold the body in stillness for 8 seconds, before you slowly exhale through the nose with control. Repeat this for 3-5 minutes.

Alternatively inhale for the count of 4, hold for 4, exhale for 4, hold for 4, and repeat.

If you find the 8 second hold easy, try 10-15 seconds hold, before the exhale, and challenge yourself to slow down the inhale and exhale.

We focus on the breath to reduce stress directly; it keeps the mind focused by using the breath as an anchor to the present moment.

Studies at trinity college institute of neuroscience, led research on the impact of breath both reducing and lowering stress. With great evidence suggesting that the breath directly influences our attention. When we are stressed, too much noradrenaline is produced by the body, making it hard to focus. By utilising the breath in mindfulness or pranayama we can reduce stress and anxiety. We also know the amygdala (the panic button in the brain) is activated by quick breathing, which means controlling the breath can have significant positive effects on the body and the nervous system.

Think about a time you have almost come into danger—that split second you slip on ice or a wet floor—we instinctively hold our breath before taking a sharp inhale. Your body is trying to keep you safe and protected, inhales take oxygen straight to the brain, to keep the mind sharp, to focus acutely on the moment. Now think about the aftermath, if you were to recover with short, sharp panting breaths, your body believes it still should be on standby for attack, with anxiety running high. On the reverse, if you instantly take long slow breaths, the body will recover quickly.

Our parasympathetic nervous system (PNS), is active

when we are at rest, keeping the body calm and relaxed.

Our sympathetic nervous system (SNS), is the system that raises our heart rate and blood pressure, working on the fight-or-flight response. Stimulating the PNS overrides the SNS, as they do not operate at the same time. Your inhales are linked to your SNS, it keeps your mind sharp, your exhales are linked to your PNS. When feeling over-whelmed, it is the slow exhales that will help you recover faster.

Activities that engage the parasympathetic nervous system help reduce cortisol created by the body. Cortisol is often referred to as the stress hormone, as it is released by the adrenal gland when triggered by an active sympathetic nervous system. This book shares many ways to stimulate your PNS.

Affirmation for Anxiety

I have anxiety; I am not an anxious person.
These emotions just are, they are not who I am.
I release stress with every exhale.
I release emotions that no longer serve me.
All that I need is within me.
I am safe and grounded.
This is temporary, this will pass.
When I live an aligned life, honouring my needs,
my anxiety is reduced.
My feelings are valid.
I can observe my thoughts without absorbing them.
I am not defined by my past or an opinion.
I am in control of my feelings.
I feel free of anxiety.
I approach my anxiety with logic.

Styles of meditation

Mindfulness meditation

An example of a mindfulness meditation is savouring a meal. As you prepare a fresh meal or fruit snack, hold each item in your hand, and honour its journey to you. Imagine you have a nice fresh pomegranate or a butternut squash, hold it, notice the weight in your hand, imagine the country in which it grew, and in which conditions? Did it need beautiful sunshine that invigorated it with vitamin D? Did it grow in the ground or on a tree? Who picked it? Who nurtured it and kept it safe and unbruised before it made its way into your home? Maybe you think back to the experience of choosing this item in the store. As you prepare this ingredient, notice the sensations, textures, and smells. Maybe you use a knife or peeler, maybe you tear it with your bare hands. What colours are most noticeable? What are you drawn to as you look at this fresh ingredient? As you come to eat this fresh food, sit nicely – without electronic noise or distractions, maybe sit outside or near a window. Try to really absorb and savour the first 3 mouthfuls, rather than eating to fill a space in your belly. Become aware of the flavours on your tongue, the textures. Really chew the food purposefully, try to stay focused on the food, see if you can keep the mind from wandering.

Notice how enjoyable and nutritious a meal can become, rather than smashing a pre-packaged processed sandwich on the go between meetings and chores.

Shower meditations

As you shower and the water connects to your body, imagine the water as a bright light of healing energy, let the energy flow over you, washing away your worries and stress.

Walking meditation

Take yourself outside, ideally in nature although any setting is fine. First stand still and become aware of your feet, and how they feel. Rock forwards and backwards gently from the heels to the toes to find your neutral stance. Start to walk slowly, being aware of the sensations in the feet and in your legs. Notice all the little details, how your clothes feel as you move, any awareness in the legs, any breeze or warmth you feel. Alternate between walking slow and controlled, to extremely slow, staying curious and aware of sensations.

Moving meditation

Find a space you feel completely yourself in, maybe a room of your home or even outside, pop your headphones on and just move your body with intuition. Through dance, yoga, or your own organic movement, let go and allow your body to take over as you lose yourself in the music. If you feel comfortable, close your eyes as you move in a way that honours your body and feels natural.

Mindfulness 3 easy ways to become present in under 5 minutes.

Details of a picture

Find a picture or a photo, that has quite a lot going on visually. Sit and study the photo to see how many tiny details you can notice. You may choose to start methodically in the top left corner, and move across, much like an archaeology dig, you may prefer to allow your eyes to become drawn to areas naturally. Really study, look for details you may never notice, maybe a tear or loose hem on the fabric in the photo, or the soft shading of a flower. Challenge yourself to see something that you would normally overlook.

Soles of the feet

Focus on the soles of the feet. First the left, and then after some time, the right. Notice any sensations, are you aware of your socks or shoes, or the feel of flooring under bare feet. Observe every sensation in the ball of the foot, the arch, the heel. Now move your attention to the toes, see if you can move your toes independently. Look for subtle differences between each foot.

Listening exercise

Listen to a song or video that has bells chiming, as you lay with eyes closed in a comfortable position, pay attention to the sound of each chime of the bell. Really listen to each chime. Listen to the ringing of the bell, when you can no longer hear the ringing, gently lift a finger to acknowledge that it is no longer auditory. Repeat with every chime.

This also translates, and can be activated, by being

intentional, eating intentionally, or doing an activity or chore without distraction. Think about cooking a meal – you have many components, and you have to time it just right, so we lean on past habits and memories to complete the task. It's a whirlwind of activity and at times we may get flustered. To be mindful, would be to isolate a part of the task and to be fully present and aware. Maybe the act of cutting a tomato – noticing the texture in your hand, observing how the knife slices through the soft skin, noting the temperature of the tomato, the scent, this is acting with intention rather than past habits.

Mindfulness is also created through acceptance, awareness, and presence.

Affirmation for Inner peace

I deserve to relax without guilt.
I know myself, my worth, and my value.
I can release emotions and thoughts that no longer serve me.
I accept myself unconditionally.
I am aligned to my soul.
I have a purpose.
I choose faith, not fear.
I protect my peace.
I am proud of what I have achieved so far, I am connected to the divine universe.
My mind is calm.
I honour my desires.
My breath flows freely.
I am free of resentful thoughts.

Reducing anxiety and raising vibrations

I love that we have finally got to a place where anxiety is recognised, mental health days and talking about struggles are encouraged, and the stigma is fading. You can easily find a thousand memes or humorous videos about anxiety, there's tips on how to ease anxiety, yet there isn't much information about how to recognise the root cause of your anxiety. Anxiety today is so prevalent that it's almost expected that everyone should have it. We are mis-sold environments that keep us in heightened states of anxiety to the point that we accept this is how we should feel daily. It is not until you allow yourself to step back that you can recognise these states. I have experienced anxiety at many levels, I have had panic attacks, I have had days where I felt so overwhelmed, I became numb. I have spent days in bed, drained, without the desire to respond to questions from loved ones. I once found myself unable to get off the floor for almost an hour. I just laid there in a foetal position, my vision blurring in and out of focus. Mostly, I existed in a heightened state of anxiety that I was unaware of. I spent years, decades actually, in this state of high alert, constantly engaging in activities to keep me too busy to analyse what was going on.

I became acutely aware just how much I operated from this place when I left the full-time corporate role. I still pick up some consultancy work, only taking ad hoc part time projects that are aligned with my values. I was in the middle of one of these projects, and for numerous reasons I was about a week behind schedule. I was getting ready to meet friends for lunch, when the owner called to discuss the timeframe, and gain clarity on next steps. A completely reasonable, if not intense call, that was about an hour long, involving many call to action points for me to execute. I had partaken in a thousand of these calls before, this was not a new world to me, but I came off the phone wired. The goalposts had moved, and I had so much to execute in a short time. My mind started racing with action plans, analysing schedules, considering hurdles and potential risks. I am now late for lunch; I turn up completely preoccupied with this project. I then ended up taking another call from the owner as I walked into the restaurant, one that caused blind panic due to an error that caused financial loss. Shit. I must fix this. I dashed inside, made my apologies to my friends, asked them to order for me, and off I went to make calls to save the world. Thankfully, this financial loss was not actually caused by an error on my side, yet I still needed to rectify processes. I felt sick and overcharged, I needed to act quick to be able to switch off and relax. I went back into the restaurant. I cannot tell you what I ate or drank. I cannot remember any of the conversations with my beautiful friends. I was not present at all. I left quickly and fell back into work.

The same evening, a little more in control now, I reflected on my day, that situation, really hating how I felt earlier. Then it hit me. Shit. I used to feel that way every day. Every. Day. For years. A continuous cycle of on the go, meetings, heavy workloads, overcrammed schedules, and lunches I was not present for. Looking back, I purposely engaged in activities to keep my mind so busy that I couldn't acknowledge that I had anxiety, instead I used it as an energy booster, a very damaging one. I would ignore emotions, too scared to sit with them. Silence made me angry. It was a well-known thing amongst my circle, that I always had to have noise.

There are so many things that we do to numb ourselves, to avoid feeling our emotions.

We drink.

We fuck.

We overwork.

We hit the gym too hard.

We pack out our schedules.

We medicate.

We use drugs.

We overstimulate.

We overspend.

We oversleep.

We overeat.

We don't get enough sleep.

We drown ourselves in noise.

We lie to ourselves.

We ignore warning signs from our body.

We justify our behaviour.

We avoid things that force us to reflect.

We deny ourselves radical honesty.

The worst thing is, that when we ignore symptoms of anxiety, we don't allow ourselves to understand or acknowledge when we feel anxious, which can lead to perceptions of poor behaviour. Not all symptoms of anxiety are palpitations, sometimes it manifests as snappiness or irrational behaviour. Turns out you might not have been a bitch for no reason, you may have been experiencing anxiety. By understanding our symptoms, you can get closer to finding the root cause of your anxiety, in turn, taking you closer to a state of inner peace. You may choose to share these symptoms with close ones, so they know how to support you and recognise when you may need more kindness.

Here's a list of some common symptoms of anxiety – of

course this list is not exhaustive.

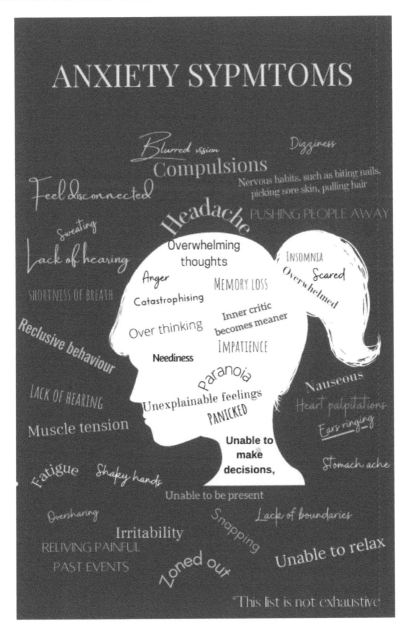

Know that it's common for most people to experience this at some point, reactions and responses just vary. Even that person you think has their shit together will experience anxiety to a degree you would not believe.

Anxiety or excitement?

On the flip side, excitement holds many of the same symptoms, the butterflies, clammy hands, and sometimes nausea or excess energy. Anxiety and excitement hold many core expressions. If you knowingly suffer with anxiety, it's important that you find time to explore "is this anxiety or excitement?" Especially in the lead up to social events. If you are starting to believe you have anxiety as it gets closer to an event, before you cancel, try to check in with yourself and see if the nervousness in your belly, the excess energy, and the racing heart, is indeed anxiety, or excitement.

Anxiety or stress?

Anxiety is often confused with stress, stress can cause anxiety, and both can result in the need for medical attention. Stress is mostly created by external factors, whereas anxiety is internalised and less easy to articulate the cause. Stress will fade when the situation passes or is restored, yet anxiety lingers on. Anxiety can be created when needs are unmet, either consciously or unconsciously, and when you deny your truth. Anxiety thrives when you are out of touch with yourself and living unaligned with your values. Anxiety is often a fear of something that will or won't happen.

Tips for anxiety

Create your own gratitude list – there are tips in this book.

Self soothe, stroke your skin, hum to yourself, hibernate under soft blankets, suck your thumb, anything that you find soothing.

Move your body in rhythm to your breath, or a piece of music you enjoy.

Scents – spray your fav scent or smell a familiar piece of fabric from your home.

Distract yourself, particularly great if you are in the throes of a panic attack. Find 5 things you can see, 4 things you can feel, 3 things you can hear, 2 things you can smell and 1 thing you can taste.

List how many colours and shades you can see around you.

Journal.

Doodle.

Stroke a pet or soft toy.

Spend time in your allotment garden, even watering house plants.

Switch off electronics and have time away from devices.

Read a physical book.

Get crafty or creative.

Lay on your back for some yoga nidra or guided meditation.

Practice mindful, conscious breathing.

Have a bath.

Grounding activities – listed in this book.

Be near water a pond, water feature, lake, or river.

Wash 3 dishes mindfully.

Moisturise your hands, feet, or body slowly.

Light candles and enjoy the ambience.

Self-massage.

Change into soft, unrestrictive clothes.

> *"Worst case scenario, you shit yourself and die"* – Robbie Cato

This quote sounds so harsh, but so often we catastrophise situations in our head.

This isn't the worst thing that will happen to you. I'm not talking about ignoring your trauma or upsets, or remembering someone always has it worse than you, but when you have an issue – that anxiety, the shit day at work, everything is catastrophised. Pause – take those deep breaths into the belly and ask yourself *"is this the worst thing that will ever happen to me"?* Yeah, it sucks that work went Pete tong, yeah it sucks you have to pay out to get the car serviced or you said something embarrassing, but really, and be honest with yourself, Is this the worst thing that will ever happen to you?

In 5 years', time, will you still be upset or affected by this issue? If not, how can you practice nonattachment?

You are resilient and powerful.

Name it to tame it.

Name it to tame it, can be used to articulate and address any strong emotion when it becomes all encompassing. You can apply the theory to the cause of your anxiety. Naming the root cause allows your mind to acknowledge your concerns and worries, in turn allowing you to analyse solutions. Explore why you are feeling anxious. Was there a specific trigger? What is the very root cause of your anxiety at this moment in time, even if you feel it sounds silly? Really dig down and keep asking yourself, "why though?" Review the scenario and inner dialogue that follows to get a sense of what I mean.

You wake up feeling anxious – you explore the cause; ah you say to yourself its work.

OK – Why though?

Well, you say to yourself, I guess I am worried about the project I am working on.

Great, why though?

Hmm, the timeline is making me nervous.

Why though?

I have been delaying the start.

Why though?

Mmm, I guess the topic doesn't excite me, so I guess I am a little worried it won't be my best work.

What does that mean for you?

That they might see me as an imposter, or they might not like me, I might get told off, I might fail. Yes, I am worried about failing and getting told off.

Why though?

I don't like being told off. Sometimes I act in a way that is guided by a need to avoid being chastised.

The root cause of the anxiety was deep rooted in a dislike or fear of being told off. Acknowledging this, lets you address internal fears and concerns at a deeper level. By articulating the cause of anxiety, the blurry sensation of feeling out of sorts and wired dispels. You can then confide in loved ones for their support and create a plan of action to tackle the project.

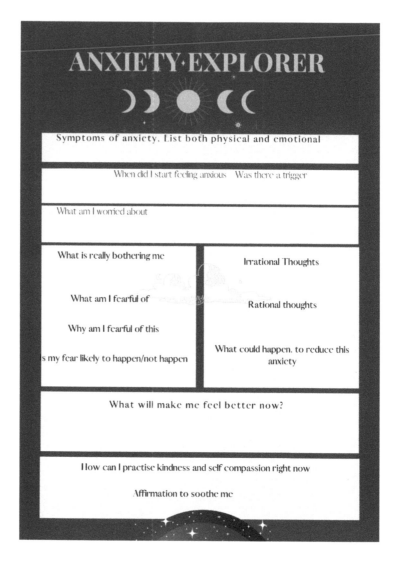

ANXIETY·EXPLORER

Symptoms of anxiety. List both physical and emotional

When did I start feeling anxious   Was there a trigger

What am I worried about

What is really bothering me

Irrational Thoughts

What am I fearful of

Rational thoughts

Why am I fearful of this

Is my fear likely to happen/not happen

What could happen. to reduce this anxiety

What will make me feel better now?

How can I practise kindness and self compassion right now

Affirmation to soothe me

Activity

Spend 5-10 minutes journaling how anxiety impacts your life and if there was a solution to your anxiety, what would it be? What would have to happen for your anxiety to fade away?

Highly sensitive person

Oh, sweet one I am sorry you carry this burden to bring

sunshine to the rest of the world, you are gifted and need-ed. The world needs your charm, do not allow the rest of us to dim your light when we do not know how to truly cherish you. You nurture others in a way we cannot comprehend, you feel so deeply, and your compassion has evolved to a deeper layer than we could ever imagine understanding. You are a rare unique soul. I hope you know how special you are and that you always surround yourself with souls who support you and hold safe spaces for you to thrive.

Allow yourself to be authentic. By mimicking others or acting with the perception of the person you want to be is exhausting. Own your beautiful and unique charms and flaws. Surround yourself with people who love you, not de-spite these quirks, but because of them.

Believe in yourself when you are highly sensitive, allow yourself to feel without guilt, this is who you are and your charm, recognise the benefits of being sensitive. You are a sought-out soul, people gravitate towards your loving kind energy. This can of course have its challenges as you are such an empath, find ways to reflect on this emotion, your own, or theirs.

Some dominant, impatient people in your life, may show frustrations towards you at times. Please know, this reflects their challenges, rather than you. Try not to apologise or feel guilty for how others act or respond. Instead of saying sorry for holding you up, try saying thank you for being pa-tient with me.

Imagine you overheard someone apologise for having a big kind heart, you wouldn't stand for it, show yourself the same compassion you do for others.

Coping techniques for Highly Sensitive People

Have a heartfelt purpose, whether it is in your work, crea-tions, or an activity – find it, lose yourself in it – it will drive you through dark times or sleepless nights.

Have freedom and flexibility in your schedule – not only for allowing time to build confidence to leave the house, but to allow additional time to feel emotions that you had not anticipated in your day. You feel things deeply, it's ok to be profoundly moved by an advert on tv or hearing a stranger's sad story. This also means you may need to carve time to allow yourself to make big decisions without the extra worry of a deadline. There's a decision worksheet at the end of this chapter, that you can use. Be kind to yourself with the length of time you may need to make a choice, however big or small, you weigh things up more than others do.

Surround yourself with respectful people.

Get your sleep.

Be creative.

Busy schedules can be overwhelming, highly sensitive people feel more. Fully immersing in moments, coupled with a natural appreciation of beauty, means that activities can take up large chunks of time. Allow yourself these moments when planning your time.

Know that being highly sensitive is a gift and a responsibility.

Be unapologetically authentic. When we do not live in alignment of who we are, and our values, we run the risk of heightened anxiety.

You are prone to over stimulation and overwhelm – travel, change of environment even restrictive clothes can trigger. Try to take time away from stimulants, people, electronics, artificial lights. Embrace the need to spend longer planning travel, or new activities. The research and time will ease you.

When you are feeling over stimulated, try changing into a loose-fitting, comfortable outfit and settle into a cosy area. Sink into comfy fabrics and soft lighting.

Know that over-thinking does have its benefits but focus on your breathing when you are overwhelmed.

Share your gratitude for life – you may have unexplainable reactions to beauty – what a way to be able to practice gratitude and share with the next generation or your friends. You have a wonderful talent of articulating beauty, in a way others cannot capture. Invest in the time for this magnificent practice.

Have small statements you can practice, so that when you are in uncomfortable situations, you honour your voice. Specifically, statements to help you assert yourself when you pick up on uncomfortable vibes. "I do not feel comfortable discussing this right now, please can I come back to you on this?"

"I would feel better if I had some time to ponder this decision."

It is healthy to honour your thoughts, emotions, and values.

Know when to seek advice from friends or therapists – you are loved and supported, even when it may not feel that way.

Consider to whom, you turn to advice. Who can support you best right now? I see time and time again strong, smart women turning to dominant characters for advice or reassurance, even when they know this person will not provide them the response they need. It's great to have confident souls who show you your blind spots, however, be sure about who it is you need and in which situations. You don't need to confirm or validate your plans and ideas to anyone.

Honour your sensitivity – hold space for yourself, become aware of your values so you move aligned with them rather than creating more internal angst. These emotions are your own, acknowledge them, observe without judgement, or guilt, and let them pass – emotions are just visitors.

Self-care is important.

Spend time with your sunshine crew, the beautiful souls who make you feel radiant.

Know that you may need more down time than others, this is ok.

You are an empath; people will turn to you for guidance and comforting words. Your sweet nature means you are a natural sponge, absorbing the emotions of others, recognise whose feelings you are feeling.

Act when someone challenges you as sensitive to justify their poor behaviour. Find a way to show them this isn't ok. You can use a prepared assertive statement, or address it in a letter or a conversation over coffee. It's ok to revisit conversations that have hurt you.

Utilise the grounding and anxiety coping skills in this book.

Recognise and respect your intuition – we feel anxious when we don't. Intuition is your brain sharing information with you, it believes you need this info to be safe or to do well, ignoring it stresses the body. Imagine your intuition is the same as when you shout, "he's behind you" in a horror film, and then get anxious when the leading star doesn't listen.

Become aware of your body – yoga and/ or meditation will help, as they create an awareness of your body. You become so in tune with your body that you can begin to notice your body's first reaction to events and statements.

Third eye activation.

Eat clean.

Exercise.

Be outdoors.

Reduce caffeine and notice your diet to stimulants.

Acknowledge your feelings, don't shy away from them, or try to numb them, just try not to become too absorbed either.

Use the RAIN acronym as below.

The RAIN acronym was first coined by Michelle McDonald. It's a system to utilise in troublesome and emotional times.

R – recognize what is going on. Can you name your emotions?

A – acceptance, allow the emotion to be there, just observing, without absorbing.

I – investigate with kindness, notice the thoughts you are having.

N – non-identification; try to witness the experience without attachment. You are having sad thoughts; you are not a sad person.

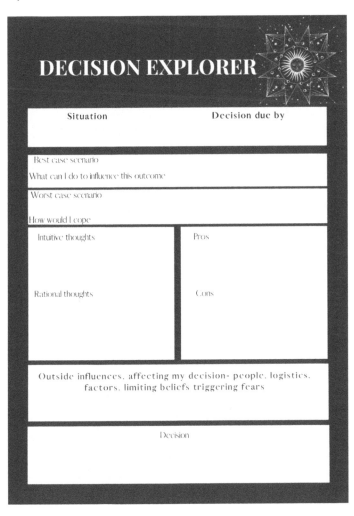

Intuition

Intuition is the link between our conscious and subconscious brain. It's our Spidey senses, the feeling that guides you, that you cannot articulate.

Our left hemisphere of the brain is our logic, its facts, language, and data. Our right hemisphere is non-verbal, it's our creative side. Between both hemispheres is the corpus callosum. Women have a thicker corpus callosum, which allows us to navigate these instinctive, swift, intuitive decisions with greater ease. Women are more inclined to state, "I just have a feeling". This can be seen as reacting emotionally, yet it is not the case, it is indeed your intuition guiding you. As our right side is non-verbal, it translates emotions and sends signals to you with symbols, images, and pictures. It's why we sometimes "just know".

It also has the ability to pick up on subtle details at such a speed they do not register as fully formed thoughts. An example would be, someone asks you to move forward with a new partnership, or a project and you have a random image – maybe something positive like a beautiful sunrise or luscious green field – an image that sparks joy. Or, you may have an image like a car crash and a feeling of dread. This is the right side of your brain conveying thoughts with you.

Have you ever met someone or had an interaction that left you feeling uneasy, that you can't understand why? Maybe that person was kind and said all the right things, but something felt off? This may be your right hemisphere picking up on tiny facial tics, subconscious movements, or remarks from that person.

As men have a thinner corpus callosum, they rely heavily on data and information from the left hemisphere, meaning they side with logical thoughts and feelings.

The scared ego stops us listening to our intuition, intuition can be perceived as risky, due to lack of evidence to support decisions or statements. You cannot articulate intuition, it's a deeper sense of knowing, it is not a fact with data backing it up. Ultimately intuition is a thought or emotion perceived as to be without evidence. An intangible thought.

You may already feel very connected to your intuition, easily trusting your gut feelings, therefore feeling confident to make seemingly irrational decisions with great results. For many adults, the thought of making a decision without facts, is terrifying. Einstein often spoke of intuition and summed it up perfectly with, *"I know what I am doing is right, even when there is no reason to believe it."*

Signs of strong intuition

Thought's pop into your head, seemingly from nowhere.

People turn to you for advice and guidance, as you are often right about intangible things.

You get people – you have a natural instinct for the nature of people, if they will be great for a particular job, if you are right to not share information with them etc.

You are frequently drawn to things unexplainably.

You often have physical symptoms linked to thoughts – feelings in your chest or stomach, or a sense of peacefulness.

You are happy even when you've made a seemingly ludicrous decision.

Heightened states of bliss or unease, without reason.

You feel safe and content when others feel uneasy or anxious due to a situation.

To develop your intuition

Seek out peaceful situations to give you the answer. Quiet allows the intuition to speak and be heard, remember it's non-verbal so pay attention, if you are overstimulated – you won't know which vibe is yours. Be open to images as answers to questions you ask yourself.

Notice your energy around others, observe how your body reacts to certain people.

Doodle without an objective, so that you can capture your thoughts as images.

Journal without restriction, reflect on your musings.

3-minute meditations – quiet the mind and the soul will speak.

Know that not listening to your intuition can cause stress and high anxiety.

Instinct is not intuition, instinct is to keep you safe, intuition is bold and guides you, helping you make that leap of faith. Think of starting a business – instinct tells you what if blah blah blah, intuition knows you are destined and bright and capable.

"The intuitive mind is a sacred gift, and the rational mind is a faithful servant. We have created a society that honours the servant and has forgotten the gift."
– Einstein

Vibrations

Everything on the planet has a vibration, this is a scientific fact. Sound is just a vibration. The water you drink, the water you bathe in, the clothes you wear, the laptop you work with, the book you are reading, the entire universe holds its own vibration. Ours is special because it changes multiple times throughout the day. Our vibration responds to sound, sight, words spoken, smells, emotions from other people, and our own thoughts.

Doctors and scientists have spent decades dedicated to the research of the vibrations of emotions. Essentially, it has been successfully proven that each emotion has a vibration or frequency. When we say low vibration energy, science backs it up. At the bottom of the scale sits emotions, such as greed, anger, grief, shame. In the middle we have contentment and at the top of the scale, the high vibration emotions are love, gratitude, elation and enlightenment.

The top of the scale emotions, such as joy and ecstasy, are huge carriers of life force and energy. It's a vibe. When you embrace these emotions, and energies, you naturally share the vibration with those around you. In the same way low frequency moods are contagious. You hold the power to impact the frequency of others, and the energy in the room.

In turn these vibrations and documented emotions, dictate how you view the world. It's the epiphany you needed. It makes complete sense. You know that when you feel a bit down, you view the world from a morbid perspective, vs the days you feel amazing, nothing can get you down, you see the beauty and positivity in everything; the stuff that might normally annoy you, simply doesn't bother you. It simply is.

What lowers vibrations?

Thoughts activate and influence our own vibrations, you have the power to influence other people's vibrations, the same way that they impact yours.

Negative thought: I believed it so deeply it became real.
Positive thought: I believed it so deeply it became real.
The choice is yours to make.

Try it, remind yourself of a good memory – really feel it, take yourself back, remember the smells, the sounds, the emotions, the joy, cherish every little detail. Spend time in this memory, now notice how you feel – maybe your posture has changed for the better, you may feel that its lifted your spirit, you may even be smiling. Now imagine you had done the same with a sad or bad memory, you would be left perhaps anxious with your heart racing, jaw clenched, frowning, maybe even tears, and a slouching posture. This is an example of how thoughts affect our vibrations. Not just your own, but others will impact from your vibes too. Have you ever noticed how a person can change the energy of the room – can either make or break an event or get together without even really doing a good or bad act? It's simply their energy that affects others.

When we operate from negative emotions (anger, jealousy etc.), we lower our vibrations when we hang around others with these traits. Some people are draining right? This is a sign they are lowering your vibrations by sharing their own. On the plus side, some people are pure sunshine and will lift yours.

It's important to recognise the need to protect your vibe as much as you do your work, others may not be so willing, they cling to these low-vibe emotions like a security blanket. In their perception its best for them when you feel the same dark way they do. Unfortunately, you may find it unavoidable to distance yourself from certain low-vibe people, it may be your job to help others who live in worlds of sadness, maybe a foster parent or a DR, perhaps your boss or even your parents or family members may be sitting at the lower end of the scale. Being aware allows you to create positive habits to reduce the possibility of you becoming affected. You may simply refuse to absorb their negativity, recognising their hurt or frustration at the world, observing it without absorbing it. You may schedule certain high vibe activities for you to do together, or for you to slink off and do afterwards. You may notice that you want to create boundaries or distance yourself from certain people, that's allowed, it's ok. It's unhealthy to make yourself spiritually available to everyone.

Unpopular opinion, but you do not owe an explanation to someone you no longer want in your life, the same as no one owes you one. Whilst I do not suggest you turn your back on a loved one who is going through a hard time in their life, you can share your knowledge and hold their hand as they navigate their troubled waters without feeling drained or trying to avoid them. You may recognise that you yourself have experienced periods of low vibrations, and that someone special held your hand and loved you fiercely throughout. Drop them a text and say thank you, express your gratitude to that magical soul.

Toxic positivity

We don't vibe with toxic positivity. If you haven't heard of Toxic positivity, it's the BS "good vibes only" tribe. It is not helpful or kind to dismiss others feelings of sadness. Whilst we want to recognise when our own vibrations are low, it is important to work through those emotions, so that we can heal and grow. Other examples of Toxic positivity are statements such as, "Just don't stress about it" rather than asking how they can help. Comments like, "winners only" suggests that the journey and growth through error and failure is not normal, when it's fact that that is where you find the magic and resilience.

They are denying genuine human emotions and providing unhelpful statements that will not nurture you through challenging times. Someone who operates from Good vibes only and refuses to welcome other emotions, is in denial and suppressing their own feelings.

Things that lower your vibration:

Junk food
Technology
Toxic people
Negative thoughts

Miswanting

Resentment

Anger

Over stimulated areas – artificial light, multiple noises, etc.

Not dealing with hurt

Living out of alignment

Not honouring your needs

Lack of self-care

Lethargy

Not moving your body

We operate at high frequencies when we move with love, gratitude, empathy, and joy. Grounding practices also raise vibrations, as does the right food, the diet we feed our brain as well as the TV we watch, the books we read and acts of kindness.

"Vibration is energy. Your thoughts begin it, your emotions amplify it, and your actions give energy momentum." –Author unknown.

The 3 gunas

The gunas are qualities documented in ancient Sanskrit in the Vedas that affect our physical, emotional, and psychological state.

Everyone will move through these 3 states. We transition and float between these gunas in the same way seasons change. There will always be one guna dominant at any point of time. From Rajas comes awareness of this, and from awareness comes the ability to change. These gunas move based on our environment, diet, and daily activities. What we ingest dictates energy, as such our state of mind is affected by the gunas. Although the gunas are very much rooted in yoga and an ancient concept, they still hold very true, particularly in this modern world.

The 3 gunas are:

Tamas
Rajas
Sattvic

Tamas is darkness. Ignorance. Hidden awareness. Downward energy flow. It is associated with the past.

When you are in a tamasic state, you may be experiencing lethargy. Inertia, unengaged with the world around you, unable to see divinity around you. You are less reactive to the world, uninterested or feeling anger. No motivation. Tamas is enhanced and brought on by poor environment – clutter, chaos, unclean areas, overeating, oversleeping, poor nutrition-eating foods that have been processed or chemically treated, alcohol, drugs.

Rajas is movement. It brings awareness. Energy change is happening in the body and mind. Caught up in the drama of the world – anxiety, passion, desire you are engaged in, and emotions associated with the future. Rajas is enhanced by loud music, over exercising, eating too quickly, spicy foods, and stimulants. It is a turbulent state.

Sattva is lightness. Awareness. Upward energy flow. You are balanced and associated with the present. Harmonious and living a calm, pure life. A clean, pure diet. Mind is clear, mentally stable and a sense of inner peace. You are not caught up in the drama of the world. Connected to the divinity.

If you imagine your mind as water – a lake, a pond, even the ocean. A Sattvic state of mind is clear, calm water – the surface is still, reflecting the beauty of the divine universe, you feel connected and at peace, in this beautifully peaceful state.

Imagine the surface of the lake now from a place of Rajasic state – the surface is impacted by outside factors – maybe heavy rain, or people throwing rocks into the water, maybe even people cannon balling. The surface is no longer still, meaning you cannot see the reflection of the divine universe, you still know it is there, but the water is turbulent, much like the rajasic mind. Tamasic state would indicate the water was so turbulent it is now muddy, unclear, thick sludge that not only fails to reflect the beauty and divinity of the universe, but you also fail to remember its existence. Dirty water sits there, muddy like your mind.

The good news is that awareness of these qualities helps us recognise behaviours, and how the world we inhabit influences them.

You can influence and change your dominant guna, in the same way you can raise and lower your vibrations.

To reduce Tamas – avoid processed foods, overeating, oversleeping, drugs, alcohol, animal products, stale, or overripe food. If you find yourself in a tamasic state – move your body, clean a small area of your home, eat nourishing foods, lay off the benders, watch your tv and diet, be mindful of those around you and the energy qualities they have.

Rajasic is the most common state. If you are looking to find Sattva, you can meditate or practice yoga, slow down when you eat, reduce stimulants around you, go outside and be around nature, keep a balanced diet and avoid overconsumption. Stay aware and connected to the divine universe by practising mindfulness and being present, avoid stimulating foods such as garlic and chilli, or too much sugar.

To achieve a Sattvic state, keep your food diet clean, as well as the information you ingest – the books you read, the tv you watch. Spend time on wholesome activities that bring you joy.

"Wisdom arises from sattva. Out of raja's greed. And from tamas comes carelessness, errors in thinking, and ignorance." –Bhagavad Gita

Grounding

Grounding – Also called earthing, is a way to reduce stress

and anxiety by distracting you from what you are currently experiencing, to allow you to process emotions in a calmer way, by bringing you back to the here and now. This can be used for PTSD, anxiety, negative triggers, or unwanted emotions, it's also great if you are feeling disconnected to the world or your own body. Grounding works its magic by overriding the panic button in your brain, that pesky amygdala, by allowing your body to respond to the present moment, rather than manifesting physical symptoms of stress and anxiety.

Grounding activities

- Journal – Journaling is writing without a framework or expectations. Rather than documenting a schedule or dear diary, journaling can be done multiple times a day, often 5 minutes is enough. Consider it a radically honest brain dump. One day may be deep emotions and the next you may write passionate to do lists.

- Be present – As tough as it is, can you just be here, *really* be here, aware of every detail of the moment without chasing thoughts and ideas.

- Dance – You know what to do, move your body intuitively, organic movements linked to your mood or breath.

- Walk barefoot – Anywhere on any safe surface, my favourite is outdoors on grass or sand.

- Be outside – Be there, without distractions, notice the gentle breeze on your face, the temperature on your skin, become aware of the light and the smells.

- Sit near a window – If the weather allows, open it a little for some fresh air and a new view.

- Laugh – Call your funniest friend, remember a hilarious memory, or watch a comedy.

- Movement – Whatever movement feels natural and calming.

- Yoga – There are so many styles of yoga. I always say yoga is for everyone, but not every style and certainly not every teacher is for everyone. Have you tried both Yin yoga and vinyasa?

- Breathwork – Try the breathing techniques in this book or guided videos.

- Mediation – Use the instructions in this book or guided meditations.

- Eat nourishing foods – Mindfully eat a high vibration food item.

- Drink water.

- Reduce caffeine – Throughout the week, especially on high anxiety days.

- Self-care – Whatever that looks like to you.

- Have indoor plants – When feeling out of sorts, tend to your plants, water them, and speak kind words that you would like to hear spoken about you.

- Visualizations – Sit or lay comfortably and visualise sceneries or images that bring you bliss. Images such as chakras, colours, waterfalls, sunsets, and beaches.

- Sound baths – Sound baths are hosted by practitioners who use crystal bowls and gongs. If you cannot attend in person, there are some great ones online. Best enjoyed with headphones.

- Play – However this translates for you, see if you can lose yourself in a fun activity.

- Practice gratitude – There's a whole chapter dedicated

in this book.

- Be near water – Or in water, have a bath, visit a river or beach, or sit near a water feature.

- Love – Love freely, fiercely and allow yourself to be loved.

- Clean your home or a small area of your room.

- Stroke a pet, an animal, or a soft toy.

- Read inspiring books.

- Light candles and settle into the ambience.

- Listen to music that calms or inspires feelings of warmth.

- Say affirmations. If you find them hard to say out loud, you can repeat them in your head.

- Star gaze, outdoors or through a window. This is trickier in high light pollution areas.

The impact of diet on our emotional wellbeing

Food has the ability to heal our bodies, keep our minds clear and stable, and can manipulate our moods and energy levels.

Think of those times you are in a rush, you have been busy all day, you're not a breakfast person, so all you've had is coffee or soda, you are starving so you grab a processed lunch, it's the closest and most convenient, you finally have food in your hands, hours after your body has indicated hunger – the food is a quick fix, but it can be detrimental. Your hunger means that you do not have the time or patience to give thanks to your food, you are more likely to eat quickly, not chewing. You need to fill a hole before you pass out and the next busy activity of the day starts. Maybe this food has additives, preservatives, E Numbers, maybe it does not even hold a single portion of your 5 a day, maybe this food is the gateway to a day of ingesting junk. You've done it now, may as well have a beige dinner too. These foods are naughty and hard to resist, even though they cause drops in energy levels, breakouts, and bloating, they can also be hard to digest. They are not nutritious for the mind or the body, they may impact your emotions.

Now think to a day you've started well – you prepared a healthy breakfast or made a smoothie – you feel alert all morning, productive and organised, your body has had a taste of nourishment and it wants more. It subconsciously starts craving more veg or fruit for the next meal. You feel fuller for longer, leaving you less likely to grab junk food. Your day, even with some naughty food or drink, has been nourished, you've drunk your water like the badass you are, your skin is glowing, life bothered you less, your mood has been stable all day, you don't feel lethargic or bloated and you sleep like a queen. I've got news for you, it wasn't because you had fewer calories – you may have even had more than the junk food days; you feel great because your body thanked you for the nourishment. There is energy in everything you eat and drink. Not all energy is good for you.

Affirmation for Calm

I am safe; I am grounded.
All that I need is within me.
Their actions are not a reflection of me.
I take time for activities that ground me.
I recognise my vibrations.
I work to create a world in which I feel safe, loved, and valued.
I seek connections, not validations.
I choose calming energy.

High and low vibe foods.
List created by
Danielle Dixon, wellness coach.

High vibe foods:

Fruits, vegetables & leafy greens (organic is best)
Fresh herbs
Spices
Nuts and seeds
Herbal teas
Spirulina
Raw honey
Beans & legumes
Water (filtered if possible and with the juice of a fresh lemon squeezed in to 'bring it alive')
Raw cacao
Unprocessed foods

Low vibe foods:

Alcohol
Animal products
Refined sugars & artificial sweeteners
Microwaved foods
Processed foods
Genetically Modified foods
Fluoride water – not filtered
Fluoride toothpaste
MSG

Caffeine
Fast foods
Processed oils & fried foods

Self-talk and inner voice

Have you ever heard someone say – "how you talk to yourself matters?" It's true.

"All that we are is the result of what we have thought,"
–Buddha.

Experts estimate that the mind thinks between 60,000 – 80,000 thoughts a day. That's an average of 2500 – 3,300 thoughts per hour. Imagine the impact those words have on our mood and energy.

A large portion of these words are action task thoughts – things you do and notice. Such as, "I'll have a shower and brush my teeth, I wonder what I will have for breakfast, etc."

"This drink tastes extra sweet today, this top feel's itchy, I should cut the tag out, my skin feels dry, I should use some hand cream."

Then there's our inner critic using non-offensive but negative language – "I must not be late, I look chunky in this dress, I always forget to turn the dishwasher on, I can't mess up this presentation today, I shouldn't have that cookie, I didn't work out today." All day long we use these soft negative words, you wouldn't talk to a friend or a child using this language, so why allow your own mind to negatively impact yourself in that way.

Imagine if you change the language, what will happen? What impact would this have on your day?

I mustn't be late becomes, "I will enjoy arriving early and having time to say hello to everyone."

I look chunky in this dress becomes, "This dress really flatters my arms and I feel confident in it."

I always forget to turn the dishwasher on, now becomes,

"It is going to feel great coming home to clean dishes."

I can't mess up this presentation transforms into, "I have worked hard and prepared for this presentation, I am looking forward to sharing my hard work." I shouldn't have that cookie because I didn't work out becomes. "I am excited to enjoy that tasty cookie."

Notice how your energy has changed reading those two paragraphs? Did you feel anxious, angry and a bit omg that's me in the first one, maybe even ashamed?

What about the second, did you feel uplifted? Did you admire the women with the confidence to flip the script that way? It's all perception, allowing it to come from a place of kindness and gratitude rather than angst.

Whilst we are at it stop fucking apologising – instead of saying, "sorry I am late," try thanking them for waiting patiently – watch the game change as you authentically own the space you inhabit.

Have you ever had a boss ask you to complete a task, and say something dicky like, "and don't forget to add commentary on the sales report," or "don't forget to tidy up your station." I did, it used to make me so mad, I wasn't a child, I know the expectations. They hadn't even given me a chance to mess up, so frustrating. Truthfully, it would put me in a mood, and I would carry out the task from a place of anger or resentment. Thankfully, I also was lucky enough to have a couple of leaders who would use positive language, yet still ask for the same thing. They would praise and say, "I am looking forward to reading your sales commentary on the report, you have great insight and it's so valuable," or "I know I don't need to remind you to leave your station tidy, you always work so methodically, and it makes everyone's life easier." It's obvious which leaders got the best results, and although I am and was back then, fully aware it was their role to inspire, I still felt valued. I worked feeling positive and stress free.

This got me thinking into the power of positive language and the impact we have on ourselves, as well as others.

Notice how you feel when you spend time with your cheerleaders, your champions, the ones who hype you, they lift your spirits as they shower you with authentic praise.

Now notice your mood when you spend time with someone who gently criticizes you all day, nothing outrageous just constant chips and passive aggressive remarks. What's your mood, your energy, your vibration after this? It's reasonable to now realise that you have the ability to change your mood with your own internal thoughts. This may have been greatly affected by limited vocabulary, others' opinions, as well as labels and diagnoses. Think about it this way – if your vocabulary is limited you are utilising core words, giving them greater power – something as innocent as silly or stupid, when said enough, can be greatly damaging. You may have inherited someone else's thoughts or opinions and regurgitate them to yourself – a mother who always made comments about your weight, or a tendency to be late, can easily blend into the same words said to you, by you, fooling the mind into the belief it is true. You may be using a diagnosis as a characteristic, so many times I hear strong women tell me, "I am sad, I am bipolar." You are not sad – you have sadness, you are not bipolar, you have bipolar, it is not emotions or diagnosis that define you. When you allow these perspectives to cloud all others, everything you do is from a place of that thought. I am not denying diagnoses, nor am I recommending you change medications. I ask that you look at your core values and beliefs to really know who you are without these diagnoses from others or even from society. Maybe family labelled you as hard work, as being "too much," the requests were always that you dial yourself down, that you are only acceptable diluted. So, you show up daily as only a fraction of your wonderful self. The whole day is spent avoiding anything that gives them confirmation that you are indeed too much. So, you don't wear the bright outfit that brings you joy, you don't allow yourself to laugh too hard or to be silly and let go in moments of enjoyment, you don't indulge in things that you love to do, for fear people will think you are being too quirky. How draining to spend the whole day denying who you are, when in reality the ones who matter – really love to see you happy, playful, passionate, and inspired by the world. To summarise, you deserve so much more than the constant overwhelm, of having to act out of alignment with who you really are, of your limiting beliefs being validated, because your joy makes others uncomfortable. Sweet girl you are wonderful, you are enough, find the souls who adore and embrace your "flaws" as your charms and let them love you fiercely. Stop giving a fuck what the miserable people say.

There's a famous rice experiment, proving the power of words, in this experiment cooked rice is kept in 3 separate containers. Each container is sealed and kept at the same ambient temperature. Each bowl is labelled, the first is labelled to be ignored, the second is labelled good rice and the third bad rice. Every day you return to each bowl, and follow the instructions, one bowl is ignored, one bowl is spoken to with kind words ("oh rice, thank you for this experiment, you were delicious, I appreciate you). The last bowl is spoken to with bad words ("you are ugly rice, unwanted and bad, why can't you be like the good rice?")

The results show that the bad rice spoils far quicker than the other 2, the ignored bowl lasts slightly longer. If you try this yourself, your energy and intention must match the words you speak.

Actions to try.

If you struggle to say affirmations out loud, practice them, along with kind words on your plants.

Explore a thesaurus or ask your friends for their favourite words that they would use to describe you, or choose words you would like to be described as. Write down your favourite suggestions and see if you can add to your vocabulary and use it with your inner voice at least 5 times a day – use post-it notes by your mirror, so you are reminded. My favourite descriptive words are: radiant, magical, compassionate, charming, wise, warm-hearted, harmonious.

Notice your language, so that you can learn the words to avoid. Bypass words such as always, don't, mustn't, shouldn't. Replace them with statements such as it will feel great, I like, it's ok.

Become aware of triggers, what events are a catalyst for periods of severe negative talk.

Affirmation for Stress

I do not have to operate under stress daily.
I am blessed, not stressed.
I am free from stress.
I am positive and peaceful.
I recognise stress and make conscious efforts to
restore my vibrations.
I deserve a stress-free life.
I recognise my stressors and can remove myself
whenever I need.
I recognise and remove toxic relationships, with
myself and others.

Masculine and feminine energies

The whole world is a stunning contrast, full of equal but opposite forces. It's the natural balance of the universe, life has death, attraction has repeal, love has hate, day has night, and masculine has feminine.

You may have heard of feminine and masculine energy, it's less of a gender assignment and more of a yin-yang situation. Everyone always has both energies, however different situations and social influences often dictate which is dominant. We are entering a wonderful season in the world in which gender fluidity is discussed non-judgmentally. This is aiding deeper understanding of feminine and masculine energies and ways in which you can awaken traits. In fact, the beauty of the universe holds both masculine and feminine energies. The moon is considered female and the sun male. Yin is female, yang is male.

Masculine energy holds space in stillness, allowing feminine energy to bring life and movement to the world.

Both energies are powerful and beautiful, neither is better than the other. You hold the divine power to invoke more of either energy, finding that balance you crave, creating the harmony that you need to live a blissful life. You may have preconceived ideas about what behaviours or actions fall under which energy. We often feel the need to label everything, which can blur realities. A controversial example of this would be an old school idea that being sensitive is a feminine trait and strength is masculine. Culturally, you may have been raised to disregard any potential masculine energies, to suppress them with the opinion they are not ladylike.

Let's look at some typical characteristics of each energy, these lists are not exhaustive.

Divine feminine energy is seen to be: dynamic, radiant, supportive, creative, nurturing, magnetic, intuitive, harmonious, fluid, sensual, wild, free, creator of communities, cosmic, intense, illuminating, delightful, desire.

Divine feminine is described as life giving, not in the traditional sense of offspring, but if masculine is stillness, then feminine is flowing. It is life in motion.

Divine masculine energy is seen to be: stable, risk taking, dominant, assertive, task oriented, structured, disciplined, protective, certainty, clarity, awareness, direct, logical, confident, stable, strong, centred, grounded, direction, purposeful.

You can choose to evoke either energy in your private life, and into your business or work. Often, we do not consider awakening certain behaviours before entering a situation. There are times and occasions that could benefit from awakening masculine energies. On the flip side, have you been relying too heavily on masculine energies at work lately, what would happen if you drew on your divine feminine energy?

Both energies constantly flow through the beautiful body that is yours, at times you may be leaning too heavily on one energy. This may be due to unhealed trauma, an unawareness of your energies and behaviours, or a heavy phase of your life causing you to fall into a very natural if not damaging cycle. When we fall out of balance, suppressing one energy, we can respond with poor behaviours.

Feminine energy out of whack can be: controlling, needy, people pleasing, naggy, critical, self-sabotaging, seduces for power, manipulative, disorganised.

Masculine out of whack can be: unsupportive, dismissive, harsh, competitive, confrontational, boastful, avoidance, withdrawal, self-loathing, restless, overpowering, restrictive, rigid.

How to awaken divine Feminine energy

- Dance without restriction, I often find this is easier with headphones on, in a space where I feel safe.

- Create – anything and everything!

- Move organically, divine flowy movement that is soft around the edges.

- Walk barefoot, on any safe surface.

- Recognise the living beauty around you.

- Goddess pose, this is a yoga pose to awaken the sacral chakra.

- Embrace and acknowledge the feminine divinity you hold in yourself.

- Guided meditations designed for this very topic.

- Moon gaze.

- Trust your intuition.

- Love fiercely.

- Left nostril breathing – in a comfortable seated position. Close the right nostril using the right thumb, so that you can inhale through the left nostril, then close the left nostril, and open the right to exhale through the right nostril, close the right to inhale through the left again, and repeat for 3-5 minutes.

How to awaken divine Masculine energy

- Spend time in sunshine.

- Meditate.

- Muladhara chakra activation, with yoga poses for your root chakra, such as malasana or yogi squat.

- Find stillness.

- Set and maintain healthy boundaries.

- Strategise and take action.

- Be bold and brave.

- Be assertive.

- Take part in something competitive.

- Right nostril breathing – in a comfortable seated position. Close the left nostril using the left thumb, so that you can inhale through the right nostril, close the right nostril, and open the left to exhale through the left nostril, close the left to inhale through the right again, and repeat for 3-5 minutes.

Affirmations for Masculine energy

I honour my masculinity.
I am powerful.
I have the ability to change my own reality.
I am balanced and strong.
I have a warrior within me.

Affirmations for Feminine energy

I have the power to create worlds.
I am powerful beyond beliefs.
I dare to love with an open heart.
I deeply honour myself.
I have a goddess within me.

Gratitude

Gratitude is the act of being thankful for what you already have, whether that is physical belongings, unseen thoughts, the world, nature around you, or even for your health.

My friend Chris always says we've won the postcode lottery – no, not the one where you win money if you pay to play, but that we have already won the postcode lottery. We walk down our local High street together and he expresses such gratitude for where we live, and how lucky we are, that you cannot help but be uplifted by his thoughts.

Chris looks at every detail of his life as a blessing, for which he expresses gratitude. He starts from the ground up.

The Country we live in — the UK — gosh how lucky are we that we are not trying to live in a war-torn home, that we are not bombed daily, that we have never had to flee our homes to escape violence from terrorist groups.

How lucky we are that we live in a corner of the world with easy access to electricity and running water, that education is free and available to all of us.

Even better – we have the NHS, we get sick, and we are cared for, nursed back to health and just sent on our way, with no invoice or debt. What a charmed life to live.

He then looks at our local area. How lucky we are that we do not have to stay in our homes after dark, with no fear of violence or gang corruption. How lucky that our town has history and charm – that these very streets were walked by famous authors, who gazed upon the very same buildings that we are now allowed to enter for free, to stay connected to our heritage. How lucky that we are surrounded by so many talented creatives, who have opened charming shops and cafes that we can frequent. How lucky that he himself had an opportunity to open his own gym and to build this community within a community.

Chris considers himself lucky when he feels bored. He tells me, "You know why Gem? Because if I am bored, it means I am safe. There's no immediate risk to my life, my safety, it means that my belly is full, that I have known enough fulfilment to recognise when there is a lack of such. I am blessed to be bored, there's many people who are not lucky enough to feel so safe, or have so much free time, that they can be bored.

Being bored is a blessing, and an opportunity to explore passions, or to rest."

Chris is filled with gratitude for the stuff we are all guilty of taking for granted. Chris has his brain wired right – there are no miswantings, he thinks material stuff is cool, but he doesn't need it, he certainly doesn't want it in the hopes it will impress someone. I have never seen Chris covet something or compare his life to someone who appears to have more. He is grateful for his life so far, for what's around him, and the opportunities that will cross his path in the future, and as a result lives in the moment, appreciating his life, and expressing constant gratitude.

The science of gratitude

We know it feels good when others express thanks for something you have done for them or gifted them. It validates your time and effort, you may even have noticed positive feelings when you yourself take time to recognize and feel appreciative of blessings in your own life. Science has done the hard work for us and documented exactly why gratitude is good for the soul.

• Increases dopamine serotonin and oxycontin, the

happy chemicals in the brain, therefore gratitude is a natural antidepressant.

- People who express gratitude have a higher volume of grey matter. Grey matter is part of the brain responsible for muscle control and sensory perception. Grey matter can be increased, promoting self-control and decision making.

- Reduces fear and stress.

- Enhances physical and psychological health, improving empathy, and reducing envy and resentment.

- Promotes better self-esteem, resulting in a decreased desire to retaliate or seek revenge.

- Better sleep, in turn producing positive proactive behaviours, such as becoming a better team player.

- You can't feel negative and grateful at the same time.

- Strengthens relationships.

- Gratitude is a great tool to be fully present.

- Raises your vibration.

- Gratitude can help you to attract great things – the frequency you vibrate is a magnet.

- You can interrupt anxiety with gratitude.

- Gratitude leads to promoted self-esteem, spirituality, optimism, selflessness, and empathy, in turn leading to true happiness.

Moving from a place of gratitude means you naturally share good vibrations. By feeling thankful, you easily become present, resulting in genuine authentic connections. You will be less likely to be in your own head, which is where a lot of perceived rudeness comes from. Have you ever been so distracted you forget to say thank you or acknowledge someone? I have. I always liken this to those who say thanks for holding a door open for them and those who don't. That simple act or acknowledgement or not, instantly affects the considerate soul holding the door. How you respond dictates the energy you invite back and shows appreciation, who doesn't want to feel valued? Go ahead and brighten someone's day with contagious gratitude.

Like seasons, sometimes we go through phases and forget to practice gratitude. It's completely normal. Those overwhelming periods of your life, where the world is exhausting, and you fall into bed or lay awake all night, occupied with thoughts rushing through your mind, exhausting you even more. When work is too intense, your relationship is going through a tricky time, a newborn baby is keeping you up. Poorly family members, your own poor health, money worries, moving to a new house, changing jobs, caring for loved ones, too much time on social media, or toxic environments leaving you caught up in comparison. During these tough seasons, it's hard, it's oh so fucking hard sweet one to just step back, to allow yourself permission to rest, let alone time to reflect and appreciate what you have, the experiences, luxuries, and people you have been blessed with.

I can't take away life's external stresses away for you, I can only share tools to help you navigate these hard times, and to find a place where you are less affected, or not at all affected, by these outside factors. To better equip you to get back to you, the real you, not the work you, the mum you, the wife or girlfriend you, not you with a title, a role or a to do list – the real you, the you that is in love with her life, her world, the you that knows herself and loves herself fiercely, the authentic you that you refuse to dilute or apologise for.

Sometimes these seasons are unavoidable, other seasons we inflict on ourselves, torturing ourselves as if this icky feeling comforts us. Learn to recognise your triggers that force you into comparison not gratitude. It may be a person, or certain people, that has you questioning all you should be appreciating – let's say you have one of those competitive sister in laws who uses passive aggression, and her constant celebrations of her success, to make you feel anything less than the magnificent person you are, there's a high chance you cannot limit interaction with her, without upsetting your family. However, you can observe this person, less as a villain, but more as someone who has her own unhealed trauma. Imagine having to feel as if you constantly need outer validation or to put down others in order to feel valuable. Chances are she is secretly admiring you, your behaviour, your daily life, the freedom you have to not constantly please people. You may also notice as you start your shadow work, that the things you dislike in her are your own fears you project. See if you can witness interactions as if you are watching tv, without becoming emotionally attached to the conversation, what do you see? Is your perspective changing?

Are there any pre or post interaction rituals you can explore? What would be different if before interactions, instead of the time spent imaging how awful this person is going to be yet again, you choose to reflect on your great week? Of your latest accomplishments? What would be different if you wrote your gratitude list before you left the house and read it again when you return home?

If your trigger is social media – can you detox your feed? Spend time noticing if the accounts you follow inspire you, add value or a smile to your day, or whether they leave you feeling deflated. You'll know who to unfollow.

> *"Comparison is the thief of joy."* – Theodore
> Roosevelt.

When you have something you have desired for a while,

you get it, you're happy, and then someone gets it easier or a better version. If the enjoyment stopped; you act from a place of comparison not gratitude. If you have ever felt you have been influenced into wanting something, you act from comparison not gratitude, you want a bag to impress someone, rather than the belief it will make you happy. You are not watering your own lawn when you compare, and chances are you are comparing your lows to their highlight reel. Expressing gratitude for your own life, your daily activities, those around you, showing gratitude for how you love and are loved, by the delight you have for the world, will stop you comparing yourself to strangers online or Mindy down the road. You start to go deeper and as a result you view with a greater depth, instead of comparing her expensive wardrobe to yours, you start to feel grateful that you have inner peace. Rather than admiring someone's model-like body, you recognise that you would prefer to have your healthy relationship with food, that you are not judged on your aesthetics for a living, that you don't have to work out for endless hours to maintain your body. Gratitude is the antidote to comparison.

"You can't be grateful for what you have, and still want something different."

16 ways to practice gratitude.

1. Volunteer for a charity, a family member, or neighbour in need.

2. Choose 10 things you are grateful for and write why. Be as detailed as possible.

3. Sit near a window and notice the view as you breathe in fresh air.

4. Appreciate yourself, your unique charms, and talents.

5. Indulge in happy moments, allow yourself to be present

and in the moment, rather than rushing to the next activity.

6. Have a household gratitude jar to read on tough days. This is a jar of tiny notes of things you and your loved ones are thankful for.

7. Say thank you more.

8. Organise a visit with a mentor or great friend, just to say thank you and share appreciation for them.

9. Notice when you are coveting or comparing.

10. Practice radical self-love.

11. Be vocal about things you're grateful for.

12. Think back to a happy memory, indulge in the memory as joy fills your heart.

13. Use thank you notes, tiny post it notes, or maybe even send a card to show gratitude.

14. Meditate.

15. Start events with good news and celebrations, meetings at work, meals with friends, gym sessions and days off.

16. Reflect on 3 things you appreciate before sleep.

Change perspective.

It's easy to be consumed by the things we perceive as annoying or unfair. If we think back to Chris's theory of challenging our perception, annoying things can become a blessing and something to be grateful for.

My worst used to be resenting paying bills, how annoying that on payday all these large chunks of money disappear before you even wake up. I would jokingly moan to my friends about all the luxuries I could buy, or places

I could visit if I didn't have to pay bills. Someone stopped me once and said, "Well you're lucky you can afford that Wi-Fi package! I can only afford to have low data usage on my phone, so I have to use free Wi-Fi on my journeys, my neighbours just changed their password and now I can't use Wi-Fi at home, yet I am expected to respond to work emails." Boy did I feel like a spoilt princess, embarrassingly it hadn't crossed my mind that my bills *were* a luxury, and for some even the basic bills make a large dent on their income. I still have my moments and I definitely don't feel inclined to send thank you cards to my bill providers, I do however appreciate how lucky I am to be able to pay for water on demand, hot, cold, something in the middle – it's mine, I can have it whenever I need. Heating, I am blessed to pay that bill, as a natural summer baby who adores the warmth, I definitely took my heating for granted, until my boiler broke over Christmas and our incredible plumber who attended on Christmas eve could not get a part for 4 days. I had been taking heating for granted daily, not even considering the luxury it is. I had forgotten the sensation of waking comfortably in a warm house. It was so cold that it became a constant distraction from every activity, it caused a reluctance to move from any small warm spot I managed to create. It held me back from going about my daily basis. It affected my mood and attention.

I had been taking heating for granted daily, not even considering the luxury it is.

Have you ever woken up to a messy house? For sure we all have at one time returned to a messy house, man it's frustrating, all you want to do is chill out, and there's so much housework to be done, it's actually made you mad how much mess is to be tidied, but wait, you have a home? How lucky you are that you have a home to feel safe in, that tonight you won't wander the streets freezing cold, unable to have a bath and watch your favourite shows in clean comfy clothes on your comfy sofa, that you won't have to spend the evening looking for a "safe" doorway that doesn't smell too much of urine, a doorway to protect you from the bitter wind, as you only have a thin sleeping bag that is still wet from the rain last night. Imagine you are thirsty, but you're reluctant to drink too much in case you need to go to the bathroom – it's risky leaving your stuff, last time someone stole it, but you might lose this space in the doorway if you bring your bag with you, it's better to get a bladder infection. You won't sleep too much tonight anyway, it's safer to kip during the day, less chance of being attacked that way. Your house may be messy with your stuff – but whether you tidy it or not, you are safe and have somewhere to call your home.

Flip the script next time you catch yourself moaning about your life.

Annoying boss? Great that means you have a job and steady income.

Bills to pay? Fab, you're blessed with electricity, running water, Wi-Fi, and a home.

Dishes to clean? How wonderful that you have food in your house.

Flat tyre to change? How lucky you are to have a vehicle.

Food shop to do? Be thankful you have money for groceries.

Noisy home? You have a safe space, filled with people who care about you – or annoying housemates.

"If you aren't happy with what you already have, what makes you think you will be happy with more?" Roy T Bennett.

Finding joy and gratitude in the little things.

The world is full of awful things, horrible people, and sad events. It's also home to beauty, miracles, and wonderful souls. What you seek, you shall find. If you look for the bad stuff, you can find it in everything, the same for the good. Too often we look for neither, we just move through our days ignorant and distracted. Taking time to appreciate your world can change the game. I am a huge believer in finding joy and admiration in absolutely everything. Whatever you are looking at right now, besides this book, the items visible in your room or the space around you, really look and study it. Notice the details, colours, and textures, choose an item in your eyeline, now cherish it. What makes it special? How did it make its way into your home? Did you get it, or did someone pick it out for you as a gift? Can you remember the day you got it? How did you feel deciding where it would live, how long have you had it? That photo frame on the table – remember the event, those details, the smells, the sounds, the touch, remember the smile as you printed it out, think of the frame you placed it in, this frame was designed by a creative soul doing their passion for a living.

It's been created, all of it – for your pleasure, have you stopped to look at it, don't just see – lookkkkk, admire it, consider its beauty thoughtfully, recognise gratitude for these comforts.

Maybe you're on the train. How can you find joy here? Perhaps in a busker, an outfit you can admire, the design of the seat that stops you from seeing the dirt, the smile of a kind stranger, look for joy and you will find it.

I just did this activity at my desk – I have a computer with 2 screens, a printer that I don't know how to use, 2 photo frames on the wall in front and a plant and a candle to the side. I was sat on a leather chair – that I refuse to sit on nicely, I'm the scruff with the feet on the chair, the chair is now faded, and the leather base is scuffed where it catches the desk as I tuck it in. I remember buying the chair about 4 years ago, before our house had even been completed, so its first few months were spent in a storage unit. The chair annoys me and to be honest, I never loved it, but it reminds me of the excitement we had before we moved in. It makes me think back to driving a big white van from the unit to the house, everything full of possibilities, the fun of deciding the layout of where everything would live. My husband also insists on hanging a thin blanket on the back of the chair, he likes it; I think it's a pain to inevitably have to keep picking it up, as of course it constantly drops to the floor, making my workspace a mess. The frames on the wall are the same as any photo you display, you choose your favourite shot – the one you look good in, that reminds you of a day of laughter, you choose the space; you hang it nicely and then you see it daily, and it becomes part of the furniture – comfy, warming but it's just there. When was the last time you looked at your photos displayed in your home and really saw the event? Study them, remember the noises, the smells, the emotions. Who was behind the camera? Can you think back to what was said? Were you hot or cold? Is there a funny memory behind this picture? Can you evoke the same love that you had the moment that image was captured?

I laughed when he said he wanted 2 computer screens, I called him a geek, well I cannot tell you the number of times I have been so grateful to be able to split the screens. As much as I think we should limit our interaction with technology, we are indeed very blessed to have these tools available. To have them at hand to help us explore the world, thoughts, ideas, document plans and vacations, watch funny videos and store all our memories. It's ok to be grateful for technology, even if you prefer the outdoorsy stuff. I am particularly grateful for the button that dims the brightness of the screen.

The cute candle to the side was a thoughtful gift from a student, I smile every time I acknowledge its presence. It makes me think of how they felt choosing it for me, the excitement of the small business owner receiving the order and my joy opening this "just because" gift.

Affirmations for gratitude

I am grateful for a new day and a fresh start.
I am grateful for the weather today.
I am grateful for my loved ones, and how much they all adore me.
I express gratitude for the health of those I love.
I am grateful for my favourite music.
I am grateful for the freedom to travel and explore.
I am grateful for the ability to have fun and be silly.
I am grateful for the opportunity to nurture my inner child.
I am grateful for my divine connection to the universe.

Gratitude exploration ideas, prompts, and gratitude list.

If you are struggling to feel thankful, use this list for gratitude inspiration.

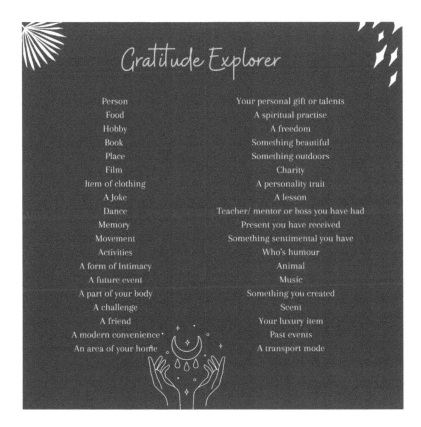

Things that you may take for granted,

Weather/season, technology, warm bed, running water, electricity, opportunities, favourite snack, healthy body, not living in a war zone, full belly, access to water, to have love in your heart, and being grateful for being a grateful person.

Body gratitude – a love letter to myself

Sit or lay yourself down somewhere you feel comfortable, make sure you feel nice and warm in unrestricted clothes. You can prop yourself up with cushions and even grab a blanket.

You can choose to play music, or light candles – allow yourself to feel relaxed and joyful.

Think of someone or something you adore and let love swirl around in your heart.

Take a deep inhale through your nose, with a smile on your face, and exhale through the mouth, allowing yourself to settle deeper into this relaxed state.

We are going to scan the body, try to allow yourself time to really enjoy this body scan by pausing to explore strong feelings of gratitude. This may be the first time you have considered your own body from this perspective. You can do a scan like this as often as you like. Many athletes conduct a brief body scan before training to check in and notice any changes in the body. Today's focus is on loving our bodies and treating ourselves with kindness.

Let's scan your body.

Start by turning your attention to your feet. You may be due a pedicure, or have chipped nail varnish, maybe you have hairs on your feet, they may simply not look how you think they should. You may even be grossed out by feet and toes in general. However, these toes of yours, well they provide you with balance and stability, if you were to lose 3 of your toes, your ability to walk would be significantly impaired. Without your toes, you would find wearing flip flops or certain shoes challenging. The arch of your foot reduces pain when on the move, your feet when bare can help ground you and connect you to Mother Earth. Your feet are full of nerves that connect you to the present moment, and to memories. Think back to the feeling of sand between your toes on the beach, to fresh cut grass tickling the undersoles of the feet, to the water in your bath or pool. The people who raised you would have kissed your tiny toes when you were an infant. Express love and gratitude to your toes and to your feet.

Let's bring awareness to your ankles, another overlooked part of your body. Your ankles provide you mobility that allows you to easily indulge in sports, dance, and partake in any movement you choose. Your ankles support you in those cute but uncomfortable shoes or heels that finish off your perfect outfit. They allow you to push off the floor in explosive movements when you need to run, to catch a train, or run away from danger or towards your child or loved one. If you have ever injured yourself, or sprained your ankle, you may remember the impact it had on your mobility. Express love and gratitude to your ankles.

Awareness now comes to your legs. Calf muscles are essential for walking and running, your knees allow you to bend down to stroke your pets, to pick up items from the floor, to change level, to climb stairs. Your thighs support almost all your body weight when you stand upright. Oh, how blessed you are, to have these active legs taking you wherever you need to go without support or assistance. You think it, they take you there. These legs that help you explore the world, that climb on tables to dance when drunk, that move freely, meaning you can wear any bottoms you choose. These legs support you in the shower, they allow you freedom of movement. I invite you to express pure love and gratitude to your legs, every beautiful inch of them.

Bring your awareness to your hips. They may be bigger or smaller than you would like, they may not be the same shape as your sisters or your friends, but your hips hold your underwear up, and they gift you the ability to run and to jump. Your hips form the beautiful shape of this vessel of your soul that we call the body. Your hips may not last your lifetime, there may be a day where the DR's step in and suggest a replacement, embrace what you have now. Your hips may have changed significantly, if you have had children – embrace your body that created life. Paint your stretch marks and cellulite with gold, move your hips to the music, led by intuition and your divine feminine energy. Send love and kindness to your hips.

Your belly – whatever the shape, however it rests when you sit down, is home to your stomach – this incredible organ allows your body to store and digest food. This means you are blessed with food in your home, that you are one of the lucky souls who can eat food of their choice, that your body aids you in digestion, that you do not know severe hunger in your daily life. Send love and thanks to your stomach, to your belly.

Bring your attention to your heart, the centre of your circulatory system, the reason blood pumps to your body. Wow here you are a living miracle – your body is keeping you alive, so that you can live your life as you please. You woke up today, and that in itself is a reason to be grateful. Not everyone made it this far. Send thanks to your heart.

Your arms – those beautiful arms of yours that allow you to pick up any item you choose, that you can wrap around your pets, your loved ones, yourself. Those arms of yours that feel like home to close people in your life. Those arms that help you dress yourself, to express your creativity with your arts, that allow you to feed and water yourself. Your fingers that gift you the sense of touch, that provide comfort when placed in others hands, to you and to them. Your hands that explore your own body sexually, and maybe your partners too. Your hands and fingers move freely so that you can do seemingly simple tasks easily – washing your hair, putting on makeup, stirring the sauce for your dinner, tying your shoes. Love and gratitude flows with thanks for your arms and hands.

Your mouth, you are blessed with lips that can smile, that can kiss your loved ones, a tongue that can taste your favourite flavours, that offers you the ability to speak freely.

Your nose that gifts you the sense of smell – your favourite scents – maybe a perfume or aftershave, the smell of certain foods, a certain person, the scent of outdoors, of laundry and sunshine, the aromas that make you feel as if you have had an imaginary hug. You smile and close your eyes as you draw your arms in close to your body, pure bliss.

Your eyes gifting you sight, maybe you need glasses or

lenses, how lucky you are to be in a corner of the world that offers opticians and eyewear – helping you to see people's expressions, laughter, smiles, sunrises, and starry nights. To visually witness the beauty of the world.

Ears that may host cute earrings, but mostly gift you the sense of sound, tuning into the frequencies of the universe, to music that brings you happiness. To be able to hear laughter and kind words.

Send thanks to every inch of your face.

Lay here, expressing gratitude for your body, this beautiful body of yours. Full of charms and unique flaws that make you irresistible to your loved ones. This body that is your home in this lifetime. Treat your body with the love, kindness, and respect it deserves. Wear the outfits that bring you joy, walk barefoot, luxuriate with your best body lotion after a long bath or shower. Use kind words when talking about yourself, to others, and internally. Teach the next generation that you are unapologetically you, embrace all that you are, so that they may too.

It's a beautiful day to love yourself and shine with gratitude.

Gratitude 14-day challenge

This 14-day challenge is a great way to add structure and to introduce a regular routine. When you start your gratitude practice, it highlights what you love the most, it shines a light in the areas of your life that your soul craves. If you haven't found yourself expressing gratitude for the activities that fill up 90% of your day, do you need to make changes? Has this highlighted something you have buried deep?

Each day you will explore a particular topic to express gratitude for.

- List your answer in relation to the topic.

- List at least 3 reasons why you are grateful for said thing/place/person, feel free to do more.

- Note the positive impact the thing/place/person creates in your life.

- Explore how your world would be without this thing/place/person.

- Journal any additional thoughts that come to the surface.

Example
Day 1 Topic – Hobby
I am grateful for my hobby of cooking.
I am grateful because this hobby:
1. *Means I can show loved ones I care, by making them nourishing, feel-good meals.*
2. *It supports my love of food shopping and buying exotic ingredients.*
3. *I love to use cooking as a form of creativity.*

My hobby of cooking has many positive impacts on my life. I find cooking exciting, the food, looking at recipe inspiration, exploring flavours and textures. It makes it easy to gather friends for events at my home, with the promise of my food. I have found it easy to bond with new people over discussions of recipes. The smell of certain meals I prepare makes me feel nostalgic and comforted. I use my hobby to prepare healthy food to support a lifestyle I choose, as well as easily making naughty indulgent treats.

My world without this hobby would be a lot of expensive, boring takeaways as I am the cook of the household. I might not feel confident to host as many events if I didn't enjoy serving food. I would maybe struggle to show my loved ones how much I care about them, or know about them, without the form of creating certain dishes. It brings me joy to feed people; I am not sure of other ways to make people as happy as I can by cooking. Food shopping would become a chore.

Additional thoughts – What would make me come alive if I didn't have this passion? Can I show love in other ways?

Try to do this first thing in the morning. If time is tight, complete it throughout the day or at bedtime, then read your list in the morning to kick start your day. I recommend sitting near a window or being outside with your favourite drink, using your favourite stationary for this new ritual.

If you can create the time to evade rushing this process, you will notice better results. Try to view it as an enjoyable task, instead of as a chore. When writing your answers, feel free to use fancy fonts and to doodle.

Topics of gratitude to explore.

1. A hobby.
2. A present you have received.
3. Something beautiful.
4. An item of clothing.
5. Someone's humour.
6. A personality trait, in yourself or others.
7. Something sentimental you have.
8. Something you created.
9. A form of intimacy.
10. A modern convenience.
11. An area of your home.
12. A freedom you have.
13. A teacher or mentor/ boss.
14. A spiritual practice.

If you are enjoying this practice and would like to consider continuing for the whole month, here are some more topics of inspiration:

15. Movement.
16. A person.

17. A part of my body.
18. A lesson.
19. An area of your town.
20. My personal gift or talent.
21. Your luxury item.
22. A transport mode.
23. A book.
24. A place.
25. A future event.
26. A smell.
27. A memory.
28. Music.
29. An animal.

"Gratitude will help you to see more beauty in the world, it can help you fall in love with the life you already have. When you have a strong gratitude practise, love washes over you, and transforms routine days into magical days,"

Chakras

Ah chakras, a word that had me raising eyebrows in my very first yoga classes. I absolutely could not connect to anything the teacher spoke about them, it used to put me off the classes. The issue was there was no mention of what a chakra actually is! I was just told to visualise it awakening as I took a forward fold, right... cheers love. Naturally, I started discovering chakras on my own terms and now I fully vibe with them. I like the magic of the chakras, and I love that science backs up a lot of theories. Science tells us that we store emotions, trauma and stress in our bodies, not just in our clenched jaws and frowny foreheads, trauma and emotion stay in our connective tissues, they manifest as physical symptoms, and won't fuck off until you address it. Good news is, there are a lot of ways to do so. Jo is much better at this than I am, so in this chapter she shares her wisdom of chakras and how to balance them.

The word Chakra is Sanskrit for "wheel". It refers to the energetic vortexes which follow the spine. Within them, they hold the energy produced by our thoughts and feelings. There are seven major energy centres in the body – they are energetic junction points connecting body and mind.

The Chakras receive life energy, known as "prana". They are not physical organs, but they do correlate closely with the body's systems. Each chakra is actually located in line with autonomic ganglia in the spine, which sends messages to and from the brain and the associated organs. Each Chakra is also linked to a colour and an element.

If you feel unhappy with an aspect of your life this could be down to a chakra becoming blocked. For example, if you are suffering from a lack of self-confidence this could mean that you need to stimulate the solar plexus chakra. If you are unable to process encounters and life stressors, they can lead to prana becoming blocked or stagnant, which can go on to manifest as physical issues. Chakra healing is a form of processing your life experiences to ensure they hold no future power.

Chakra Diet

The easiest way to boost your overall health is by eating a rich and varied diet, including all the colours of the rainbow. This is said to also balance the chakras. Each chakra is associated with a different colour and the theory is that foods of the same hue carry the same vibrations which will activate and balance the corresponding chakra.

Muladhara or Root Chakra, sits at the base of your spine. Colour is red, and the element is earth.

The root chakra is linked to basic survival needs – having a safe home and sense of belonging. A balanced root chakra is associated with having a strong sense of security, patience, stillness, and connection to your instincts.

A block in the root chakra can often be embodied as a lack of confidence, feeling unsafe, anxious, disconnected, and carrying anger, worry and tension in the lower back. An overactive root chakra displays as greed and aggression.

The root chakra can be brought back into balance by practicing grounding practices such as walking outdoors barefoot, yoga postures such as warrior poses. In chanting the sound "Lam" is used. If you are suffering from a lack of motivation and fatigue, reach for crimson-coloured foods to boost the root chakra such as beets, strawberries, radishes, tomatoes, and chillies. Garlic, spinach, and carrots also stimulate the root chakra.

Affirmation for root chakra – I am safe, I am grounded, all that I need is within me.

Svadhisthana, or Sacral Chakra, sits between the base of the spine and the belly button. Colour is orange, and the element is water.

The Sacral chakra is connected to creativity and birth. It is associated with vitality, sexuality, and energy.

A balance usually denotes a good ability to work with others, a good home life, and creativity.

Blockages may be evident in feeling a creative block, an unhappy home life, feeling trapped or stuck and lethargic. Overactive sacral chakra may display as being oversexed, guilty and materialistic.

Balance can be encouraged through the use of hip opening, being near water, or exploring your sexuality, particularly healing any sexual shame. Bright orange food stimulates the sacral chakra – if you are suffering from feelings of low confidence, reach for oranges, mango, cantaloupe, and honey.

Affirmation for sacral chakra – I honour my sexuality and express my creativity freely.

Manipura, or Solar Plexus Chakra, sits above the naval. Colour is yellow and the element is fire.

A well balanced manipura chakra will manifest as inner personal power – feeling self-confident and having an abundance of willpower.

It is linked to strong self-control, authority, and power. The Manipura is connected with laughter and joy.

An obstruction of this chakra can often result in feelings of low self-esteem, and a lack of confidence and procrastination. A key characteristic of someone suffering an imbalance of the Manipura will be apologising a lot. An overactive solar plexus chakra displays as overly critical and power hungry.

Balance can be restored with creativity, sun salutations in yoga, or direct sunlight for those who do not practice yoga. Sunny hued foods such as apricots, pineapple, yoghurt, whole grains, and cheese will lift the mood and boost self-esteem.

Affirmation for solar plexus chakra – I live an abundant joyful life and deserve happiness.

Anahata, or Heart Chakra, sits at your heart. Colour is green, and the element is air.

This chakra is linked with being compassionate and loving, and feeling deeply connected.

It is connected with the heart and circulatory system – energised with prana or life energy.

A blockage usually leads to being overly critical, having little or no self-love, and feeling disconnected or lonely. It can show as being too emotional or showing no emotion. An overactive heart chakra can show as jealousy and pettiness.

An imbalance can be resolved with practising gratitude or forgiveness, back bending positions, opening the chest – such as wheel pose or fish. Energy boosting greens will benefit the heart chakra, broccoli, kale, brown rice, and lentils.

Affirmation for heart chakra – I give and receive love freely.

Ushuddha, or Throat Chakra, sits at the base of the throat. Colour is blue, and the element can be both air and space.

The chakra of our truth and our authentic voice, the Ushuddha, or throat chakra, is linked with communication and self-expression.

It is connected with speech, sound, vibration, and communication. A healthy balanced throat chakra brings with it the power of honesty, creative expression, loyalty, kindness, and the ability the speak mindfully.

A dry throat, problems speaking out, and difficulties expressing oneself are symptoms of a blockage within the throat chakra. An overactive throat chakra may encourage gossiping and loud opinions.

It can be released with laughter, singing, yoga positions such as the camel pose, fish, shoulder stands and plough, as well as with the use of mantras and pranayama. Anxiety soothing foods such as blueberries, blackberries, kelp, wheatgrass, ginseng, and mushrooms can help to bring balance to the throat chakra.

Affirmation for throat chakra – I speak my truth and communicate with ease.

Ajna or 'Third Eye' Chakra. Colour is indigo, and the element is light.

This chakra is connected to insight and intuition, beyond wisdom.

A balanced healthy third eye chakra is linked with good concentration, wisdom, imagination, and intuition.

A lack of self-esteem and constant need for reassurance is indicative of an imbalance of the third eye Chakra. You may suffer from headaches, a wandering mind, and trouble concentrating. It can also lead to cynicism, nightmares, and a general feeling of being disconnected.

The third eye chakra can be brought into balance with meditation, stargazing, and resting in child's pose – grounding and resting the third eye. It can also be rebalanced with meditation and by eating purple foods such as grapes, aubergines, and black currants.

Affirmation for third eye chakra – I trust my intuition, the world amazes me.

Sahaswara or Crown Chakra. Colour is indigo, and the element is pure light.

It is the cosmos source of all spiritual connection and ultimate wisdom.

Connection with high consciousness – the Thousand Petalled Lotus.

This is the unification with your higher self, bringing openness to the higher consciousness.

An imbalance of the crown chakra often presents as insomnia. It can be a lack of purpose or direction in life. Feelings of confusion, alienation, and hesitation.

Balance can be brought to the crown chakra through shadow work, inversions, and lowering the head and bringing blood flow to the crown. Balance can be reached by fasting and detoxifying in order to flush out toxins, boost energy, and clear the mind.

Affirmation for crown chakra – I feel divinely connected to the universe.

Limiting beliefs

Limiting beliefs are the invisible restrictions that hold you back from the life you want, and from activities or relationships you desire. Most adults hold limiting beliefs of their own, some have been imposed from a place of love, and some have been forced upon you from a place of hurt, of someone else's insecurities and fears. These beliefs have arisen as a result of how you were programmed, commonly these are words of love shared by your guardians to keep you safe, at least from their perspective, sharing their own limiting beliefs, with the notion it will protect you. "Money is evil." "Work should be reliable and mundane, not exciting but risky." You may have slowly imposed limiting beliefs upon yourself, witnessing other downfalls or sadly, these limiting beliefs may have been projected onto you from a person of authority – such as a teacher, guidance counsellor or sports coach. The adults who feel it's ok to tell a child they will never amount to anything, that they are not smart, that they will end up in a deadbeat job. Those com-ments hold such weight to the mind of a growing adolescent, you probably even took the comment in your stride, but it hit deep on some level, so you stop trying, as they were probably right anyway. The most heart-breaking lim-iting beliefs are the ones showered down onto you from toxic relationships. Almost 1 in 3 women have experienced abusive relationships. Emotional abuse taking the form of relentless comments telling you that you are worthless, that you are unlovable, that everything that goes wrong is your fault, that you will never find love, that no one wants you, your family don't want you bothering them. Hearing fero-cious comments daily from the person who tells you they love you the most, takes its toll. You start believing what they say. Those awful words they use to keep in you their clutches start to become your perceived truth. Oh, sweet girl, you are magic, you are lovable and beautiful. You are wanted. Those awful things they tell you are the lies they say to keep you in their life. I wish you all the hope in the world that you flourish in life. You are deserving and strong.

Limiting beliefs are assumptions you have made or been told, that you now hold onto on a deep level, stopping you from living an unrestricted life of abundance and joy.

How they made the elephant believe that it is not free

The Elephant theory is a heart-breaking one. When a baby elephant is born into captivity or stolen at an early age, usually for travelling circuses or performance shows, the horrific owners tie its baby leg to a large sturdy tree trunk. The baby elephant can only walk within 1 meter of this tree trunk. As an infant it often tries to move further away, yet it does not have the strength to move this large tree trunk, rooted deep into the ground. After a while, the elephant stops. It accepts that it cannot move past 1 meter. The elephant grows and becomes mighty, yet for years it has been shown that it is not capable of moving the trunk. Its owners, now confident that the elephant has learnt its restrictions, can tie this magnificent mammal to a small bucket of water, and the elephant will not move past this 1-meter circle. The elephant recognises the rope around its leg as the truth of restriction. We know the strength of the elephant. He could effortlessly walk away, yet the elephant now holds this limiting belief – that he is stuck, that he cannot pass this invisible barrier that has been imposed.

You hold your own limiting beliefs. I am here to help you explore your own and guide you to unlock the true perspective, so you can throw off the restrictions holding you back from everything you deserve.

Common limiting beliefs.

Financial – Money is evil, I could never afford that, earn a penny spend a penny, people like me don't get rich, you cannot get rich in an ethical way without being ruthless, can't buy happiness.

Success – You must have job security, a creative role is not a job, it's safer not to go for the promotion, they will think you don't like the job you have.

Failure – The world is dangerous, not smart enough, you can't make money from your passion, people will talk/judge/wait for me to fall down, can't buy happiness.

Self – Not deserving, it's too late to change, that's not for people like me, I will fail, I am not pretty, others are better than me, I am not qualified enough, people will think I am a fraud.

Love – I am unlovable, I am not worthy, I shouldn't expect much from my partner. Everyone's a bit miserable. I am a burden to those around me. I must dilute my behaviour, so I am liked.

Health – This is just how I am, this is just how I look, this is just how I feel. I come from a family of illness, so I welcome ailments without exploring cures.

Limiting belief statements often start with:

I mustn't
I can't
I shan't
I shouldn't
I'm not
I don't

Explore your own limiting beliefs.

The danger of limiting beliefs, besides missed opportunities, is that it becomes your truth. You carry yourself as if it has already happened, to protect yourself from disappointment. This Limiting Belief stops you giving it your all, as you are waiting to be proved right, then it comes true validating you were right all along – evidence! See I told you my limiting belief was right; I shouldn't have even tried a little bit. This can even turn into resentment or anger for even trying.

Your Limiting Belief dictates how you view the world, and ultimately how you engage with the world. It alters opportunities and events.

Your limiting belief is that you are not good enough, which manifests as imposter syndrome, as a result you are reluctant to voice opinions, to make bold decisions or to assert yourself, for fear you will be outed as an imposter, that the rug will be pulled out from under your feet. This opinion holds you back from influencing a larger audience who truthfully would benefit from your expertise. I promise you, the recruitment team at your place of work, did not offer you the role as part of an elaborate prank. They saw the greatness you deny you have.

If you were to remove this belief, you would feel greater confidence in your decisions, creating more free time, you won't stand in your own way of the things you earn or deserve. Your voice becomes validated, and you no longer spend evenings second guessing yourself. You feel appreciated, seen, heard and respected.

You will by default share your Limiting Beliefs with the next generation and your loved ones. Your Limiting Belief is your perceived truth; therefore, it becomes the language you share, through self-deprecating jokes, or as statements, and reasons/excuses as to why you do not do a particular thing. Another way to consider your limiting beliefs, is as fears – it's what they are essentially. As a community we share fears. To keep the youngsters safe we tell them fire burns, do not jump from a height you can hurt yourself, don't take out credit cards you'll get in debt etc. We teach them not to take risks, so they remain unharmed and safe. Some limiting beliefs manifest as a perception of protection. "Don't take jobs with irregular income or try to start your passion business, it is better to be miserable with a regular wage." If this is your Limiting Belief, this is the language you share with those around you, don't you want to free yourself of these restrictions, and empower the next generation?

"Negative thought I believed it so deeply it became real, positive thought I believed it so deeply it became real."

How to overcome

Pay attention to your dialogue when discussing opportunities and events for yourself, notice the language you use to describe yourself. What are your limiting beliefs?

Questioning your limiting beliefs

Activity to explore – grab a pen and paper, and practice radical honesty.

1. My Limiting Belief is… (you may hold more than 1, explore them all)

2. What's the origin of this belief?

3. Is this belief helpful – does it keep me safe?

4. How do I feel when I experience this Limiting Belief?(List both emotions and physical symptoms)

5. What are the facts about this Limiting belief?

6. Where's the evidence to support this belief?

7. How does this belief hold me back?

8. Is this Limiting Belief true?

9. What would I do without this belief?

10. What would the people who love me say about my Limiting belief?

11. What would my life look like without this belief?

12. What wouldn't my life look like without this belief?

LIMITING BELIEFS

Limiting belief

Evidence to support limiting belief

Where has this belief stemmed from

How has this limiting belief kept me safe	What would my friends say about this limiting belief?
How has this limiting belief, held me back	What would my life look like, without this limiting belief?

Thank your fears and limiting beliefs, for keeping you safe, and that they will no longer serve you

New empowering truth to support the release of this limiting belief

Moving on

Thank your limiting beliefs for trying to keep you safe so far. Now tell your Limiting Belief that they no longer serve you. Allow yourself to acknowledge that you are changing the narrative.

Affirmations to support new empowering truth to counter old limiting belief, as listed below

Old belief vs new empowering truth

Create statements and supporting affirmations as your new empowering truth.

Old belief – I am unworthy.

New empowering truth – I am worthy of people's time and kindness, I have so many beautiful charms.

Old belief – I come from a history of family illness; it is natural that I too suffer.

New empowering truth – I do not have to accept illnesses, I actively seek out healthier ways of living, I deserve to live an unrestricted life full of nourishment.

End of chapter note. If you or someone you know has been affected by domestic violence and needs support call refugee for women and children affected by domestic abuse 0808 2000 247.

Affirmation for Manifesting

The universe will gift me what I desire.
The universe is aligned to my truth and my
happiness.
I deserve the life I crave.
I am worthy of this life I am manifesting.
I shall put in the work and stay clear on my wishes.
The divine universe has my back.

Inner child and shadow work

Inner child and shadow work can be extremely daunting and overwhelming, especially for anyone who has experienced severe trauma. You may prefer to explore this work with the guidance of a licensed therapist.

The term "Inner child" stems from Jungian theory, it is also described as divine child. It's the little you, and the wounded inner child. It refers to the scars you carry from events, or social behaviour from family members, the wounds are from traumatic events or moments and occasions when you were shamed for being you, when your needs were left unmet, and you suppressed emotions and desires to please elders in exchange for praise or attention.

Think back to your childhood and who was around when you were your loudest self, those living room talent shows you would put on, or repeatedly shouting, "Hey look at me," whilst you did a twirl or jump in the air. Who's attention were you vying for? Remember how they responded, were they supportive or condemning, were you completely ignored, or aggressively told to stop? How did you respond to that?

Those seemingly tiny moments have shaped you, your opinions, views of the world, and how you believe you are seen and should behave.

The biggest and most common areas of trauma, or inner child wounds are:

Abandonment – This child feels left out and lonely, and as such has a huge fear of being alone or abandoned. Into adulthood this trauma displays as co-dependency, attracting emotionally unavailable people, and threatening to leave in an attempt to manipulate and gain control of the situation; but also has a strong need to hear that the other person in question doesn't want to leave and would be devastated to lose them. They project their greatest fear, looking for reassurance.

Guilt – This child is afraid to set boundaries, a people pleaser who attracts people who make them feel guilty, they may also use guilt to manipulate situations. Prone to lashing out, afraid to ask for things or needs to be met.

Trust – This insecure child sets strict boundaries to avoid trusting others, and themselves, due to a crippling fear of being hurt, often left feeling unsafe or in an unstable situation requiring constant validation.

Fearful – This child was criticized heavily and now as an adult is fearful to engage in any activities that they were once chastised for – making a mess and being too loud or inappropriate. When this wounded inner child does not receive enough praise, it often manifests as anxiety, questioning relationships, fearing if they are liked or in trouble.

Neglect – This Inner child holds on to traumatic events, leading to low self-worth, attracting others who do not value them. As an adult this wounded inner child manifests as an inability to say no, repressed emotions, yet a regular theme of self-pity.

How do I know if I have an injured Inner Child?

You know you have unhealed trauma from your early years if:
    You deny yourself pleasure or hobbies.
    You don't know your worth.
    You struggle to control your emotions, or you're prone to outbursts.
    You can't set or respect healthy boundaries.
    You're a chameleon.
    You tell yourself lies to justify your own behaviour and that

of others.
Constantly scared people will leave/abandon you.
Put others needs before your own, in an unhealthy way.
Tolerate abusive or negative behaviour from others.
Feelings of shame on a regular basis.
You are a people pleaser.
Addictions.
You compare yourself to an unhealthy degree to others.
You don't feel safe to be you.
Tendency to form co-dependent relationships.

Inner Child healing

Good news, it's not too late to nurture or apologise to your inner child. You can acknowledge the hurt from the past, you can treat little you with the kindness you needed. Moving forward you can continue the healing, allowing yourself the things you have denied yourself. Heads up, it can get a little bumpy.

Healing your inner child can mean revisiting little you, to heal the past, awakening little you with the now, and honouring little you, moving forward.

The past

Acknowledge and observe childhood memories without absorbing the emotions you felt, can you view the memory as if you are watching tv? You may choose to witness mundane memories, or memories you automatically remember as hurtful. Be kind to yourself, seek support from loved ones and/or trained professionals if you know this journey will be hard.

Release and move forward – you may not get the closure you want, but you deserve the peace – what would have to happen for you to feel validated?

Write a letter to your Inner Child, tell them everything you need them to know.

Practice radical honesty.

Therapy – there are so many types – Jungian therapy specialises in childhood trauma.

The now

Add play and joy to your day.

Set and maintain healthy boundaries – watch out for the people around you who don't respect them.

Connect with others freely, without diluting your personality.

Be aware of your wounds, try to view present situations without the views of injured little you.

Moving forward

Ask what the lesson was in painful situations, and how you can show kindness to yourself and others moving forward.

Recognise your hurt, acknowledge the pain, explore what needs to happen to allow you to release the hurt; articulating how you will feel when you let go of these thoughts, beliefs, and emotions.

Affirmations;

I am willing to forgive my parents, they did the best job they knew how to do.

I recognise my guardians as people with their own unhealed trauma.

How I was treated was a reflection of that person, not of me, I am lovable and worthy.

I love myself unconditionally.

Speak to your Inner Child, as you would any small person.

Imagine a 10-year-old – you may choose to imagine an 8-year-old or a child of a significant age to you. Tell them they are not worthy, they are unlovable, tell them to be quiet when they express too much joy, that their mistakes are unacceptable. Cruel isn't it. You can't imagine expressing such cruel thoughts. These awful words are not true, no child is unworthy or unlovable, and that goes for you too. I am sincerely sorry for this hurt you hold in your heart, any fear that you are not good enough, that you are a pain, that you don't deserve happiness, that people leave because of you. It simply isn't true.

Imagine fiercely hugging that child. That child is now you, it is your Inner Child, tell your Inner Child that you are sorry for those unkind words. That it was hurt people projecting them, that they were never anything other than perfect and beautiful and deserving. Change the narrative – promise little you that you'll be kind, that you'll indulge in the things you love, that you'll respect your body and treat yourself with compassion. Tell your inner child every soothing word that you longed to hear.

Many adults hold inner child wounds and are unsure of the catalyst. It may not have been one extreme incident, your Inner child wounds may not have come from your parents, in some cases it's other relatives or even educational settings that had the greatest impacts. Your wounds are valid. All of them. Even the ones you feel are silly.

Even if you had a fantastic childhood, spend time on the next activity, see if anything resonates with you.

Inner Child thoughts to explore.

When did I stop having fun/being playful?
How did I express creativity as a child?
When did I start being so hard on myself?
When did I last lose myself in an activity?
What does my Inner Child need?
What needs were unmet when I was little?
What was I denied as a child?

Mother yourself

Validate your thoughts and emotions. The way you feel may

be solely from your perception, that does not lessen the weight they hold. Often you are told off for being too sensitive, or viewing a situation from your perspective, not viewing multiple opinions at the same time, unfortunately that will be true. We all view the world from the perspective of historical events that have determined our beliefs – not to trust people for they let you down, that you are annoying and should express yourself less, that you are naughty and undeserving. When you allow the narrative of others to dominate your own thoughts, you are almost gaslighting yourself. Try observing your thoughts. Why have you reacted this way? What's the root cause of this reaction? What's the fear? Why do you feel triggered? What's this stemmed from? You may be responding to a seemingly small issue from a place of trauma – you are clingy or nervous if your friend or partner does not return on time because a loved one failed to return and you feel you need control as an example.

Set and maintain healthy boundaries. Become aware of who responds to your boundaries with aggression or refusal to cooperate – this is a sign of disrespect and manipulation. Boundaries are healthy – they can cover a multitude of things, time, space, topics of conversations.

Examples of setting boundaries may be:

I do not feel comfortable discussing this with you.

I am going to sit in another room for a while, please respect this time away.

You can email me and I will respond at a time that suits my schedule.

I understand you are angry, please do not take it out on me.

I would love to come, but I cannot stay the night.

Pay attention to your needs and honour them. It is your responsibility to live a fulfilled happy life. When you take care of yourself, you take care of all of us, you move differently when you are fulfilled. You attract your right tribe when you are unapologetically authentic. Relationships deepen, and you will feel truly understood with deeper bonds. Ignoring desires, dampening your personality, playing a role, all have huge damaging consequences on your nervous system and overall happiness. Why are you ignoring your own needs? Who are you trying to impress? Think to the people you most admire. What qualities do they display that you like? What stops you from feeling like you can be authentic? You don't ignore thirst or hunger, you maintain personal hygiene, so why not continue the honouring of the body with the soulful stuff?

Praise your achievements. Now this one is tricky for women, society told us to show up and be good, but not better than them. You may have grown up in extremely competitive female circles where jealousy, rivalry, and nasty comments came after you displayed success. Ooh what about you incredible creatures who work in a male dominated industry, your achievements are often downplayed. Your limiting beliefs tell you that your achievements were just luck or the result of someone else's hard work. No babe, we don't play small anymore, own it, totally own how fucking fantastic you are. Your biggest achievement today may have been getting dressed, it may have been a creative award, an industry award, you may have just bought your first car or home. Own it! You did the hard work and it paid off! It was all you, do the happy dance, share the story with your friends, reflect on your journey to accomplishment. Bask in the celebration, before you head off to the next thing. You did great. End of.

Speak to yourself with kindness. We hear this all the time, and we nod and say yeah, I know, we tell each other to talk to yourself as if you're talking to a friend, and we say, yeah, I know, then we go and be mean to ourselves anyway. WTF. Can you notice when you use ugly words to describe yourself – internally or externally? These ugly words, do they sound familiar? Where did you learn them?

Did someone once say those exact words to you? Let's say you've just accidentally knocked something over and made a mess. What do you say to yourself? A simple oops? Or something meaner like, "I always make a mess, why am I so clumsy all the time, I can't do anything right." Are those words that were spoken to you as a child? Or maybe in a relationship? Is there truth in it? Does it even matter if there's truth in it? You're clumsy… and what? You're not a bad person, you're not malicious, you don't do it on purpose, you're not trying to hurt anyone, it can all be tidied up, is this what you will fret about on your deathbed? About that time, you spilt a cup of tea on the rug. Of course not. If you had made this mess by accident, in the presence of a nurturing maternal role, think of what this divine woman might say to you – a warm embrace, telling you it's ok, she knows it was an accident, not to worry and that you can clean it up together. The entire atmosphere of that event has changed, there's no chastising, no anxiety or anger. The mess was still made, and on both occasions, it was tidied, yet in the first scenario you felt attacked and belittled, maybe even unloved, and the second scenario you felt safe. You have the ability to cause all these emotions internally, when you talk to yourself with unkind words. Maybe now you are ready to recognise the language and tone you address yourself with.

If you find it hard to speak kind words to yourself, imagine your sweetest friend and what they would say to you, and try to repeat those kind words to yourself in your own voice.

Speak to your plants and say all the sweet words you would like to believe about yourself.

Hold yourself accountable, with compassion. We were all raised in extremely different environments, all of which have an impact. For some that can mean holding yourself to unrealistic expectations of perfection, burning out, intense gym sessions to achieve the perfect body, studying or working regularly into the early hours to be successful, only accepting perfect grades, flawless results, even at the sake of your own physical and mental health, anything below perfect can result in crushing despair, panic attacks, fear that you won't be liked anymore. These extremely high standards are often projected onto others around you, an expectation that they too should be maniacal about delivering perfection, even at the cost of your relationships at times. What a tiresome world to play a part in.

Some people were raised without expectations, an unspoken agreement that it's ok to coast through life. That there's no value in hard work or gentle discipline, this can lead to an unfulfilled life. Feelings or beliefs that certain things in life are "not for people like me", combined with a lack of accountability can leave others feeling they can't trust you to deliver on certain projects or promises. Ultimately this means that you may operate at a lower level of engagement. Two very opposite ends of the spectrum, both can be improved by accountability with compassion. Setting realistic smart goals and approaching with kindness.

Example:

The situation – you must deliver a presentation at work in 7 days, this is a 2-person job, you have been assigned a partner to collaborate with, you know this colleague reasonably well, you respect them, but you've never worked on a project together before.

The overachiever without compassion. immediately wants perfection from both parties. This presentation is important, and must become the number 1 priority, screw their family commitments and your social plans, if you both dedicate an additional 30 hours outside of office hours to this presentation, the world will see how hard you work, and your status will be maintained. It's decided you must both cancel your private life, deadlines are your thing. You know if you stay up till 1am daily you can research this topic, and create a flawless PowerPoint presentation, you need the expertise of your colleague so you set them the same schedule – X hours to research, X to gather info and then you can both import them into your flawless PowerPoint. All will be well. Your colleague pushes back, this presentation isn't their work priority, nor are they willing to take their work home, why should they? They won't get paid, and they have a busy family life. They think they can find a few hours at work towards the end of the week to research and gather data. You can both reconvene the day before its due to put it together and prepare for the meeting. This unsettles you, that's not a fair split of work, why should they get the inevitable great credit from all your hard work, you won't have enough time to perfect the delivery if you only meet the day before – *fail to prepare and prepare to fail!* You try to reason with them, but they are very aloof, and you are not senior to their role. What options do you have? They are going to ruin this presentation. You spend the next 7 days trying to over deliver on your portion of the presentation to compensate, you considered ways to professionally share their laziness and lack of commitment to highlight your hard work. You cancel all social and personal plans, and end up losing sleep from fear... wait is it anxiety? Oh, it might be anger, yeah you are angry that they feel they can relax whilst you have to bust your balls to stay in the game. Resentment rears its ugly head, and seeps into your life.

The overachiever with compassion. You still have high standards, and care about what you do and the quality of work, yet you recognise other's values and priorities may not reflect your own. In acknowledging these differences, you can view different opinions, you are not looking at your colleague with resentment, instead you are wondering if there is a lesson to learn. This person also delivers great work, yet they seem to be able to switch off and enjoy their private life. Is this person more productive at work as they have attended to their own personal needs and desires? Where can you show compassion to yourself on this project? High quality is still important to you; however, you now treat yourself with kindness, knowing that this presentation is a small percentage of your job, and an even smaller percentage of you as a person and the life you lead. Your compassion for yourself and for others means the emotion in which you approach this project is kinder. You are not fighting to work under or against anxiety, anger and resentment. *Instant win.* Your compassion allows you to recognise which personal needs you must address before starting, how much more productive would you be if you caught up on your sleep first. You know that by stepping back and enjoying a personal activity will provide you mental clarity, allowing you to not only view the work with an elevated perspective but with a greater understanding of the bigger picture, you can adopt an approach of multiple perspectives at one time. If you don't cancel your social plans, maybe you can talk with your friends, discussing your ideas for the presentation. Your relationship with your colleague will improve as neither of you are being met with resistance. Your entire demeanour on the day will be brighter and more engaging as you've allowed yourself space to drop the negative use of holding yourself accountable for unrealistic expectations.

The coaster without compassion. Same project, same colleague, same deadline. No accountability – you know this colleague is smart, great, that's half the job done, you don't need to worry really or put in much effort on your side. 7 days is plenty of time, you don't really have much in the old diary. Actually, you think to yourself, I can pull together some rough ideas – give it to your colleague, they can spruce it up, pop it in a PowerPoint, decide how they want to deliver on the day, and you can go with the flow.

There's no desire or inclination to create a fair workload with your teammate, neither have you considered your capability if you applied yourself to the project. Sure, one project doesn't matter in the grand scheme of things, but how you do anything, is how you do everything. You may not have considered that you were chosen because they love your ideas and tone of voice, that this is a stepping-stone to you discovering something about yourself that you love to do, or an opportunity to bond with a colleague and learn a new skill. Is your lack of accountability due to dis-interest in this job, the place you spend 40 hours a week at? Is there a fear of failure, or do you lack the knowledge or discipline to know how to approach this challenge? The lack of accountability and compassion affects you; you are neither engaged nor challenging yourself, you are uncon-cerned about the potential impact on your colleague and those who are awaiting a presentation. Is this a habit that shows itself in your personal life too? You still care about your job, so the night before the meeting you don't sleep that well, and you feel anxious all morning on the big day. Oh gosh, will your boss notice? What if this was a test? Should you have done more? What's your colleague going to say about you as a teammate?

The coaster with compassion.

You know that you tend to go with the flow, it's why they gave you this job – you add a great playful dynamic to the team, and a fresh perspective because you are not bogged down with the daily bores that seem to affect others. You al-ways wing it, and you are doing well so far, although it does sometimes give you sharp bouts of panic at times. You know that deadlines and detailed projects aren't your best, so let's lean on your strengths to offset that, what do I bring to the table here? Should you share with your colleague that your best work is done at the last minute so they don't spend the week worrying? Sharing compassion for yourself and for your colleague whilst respecting the goals of the business leaves you feeling proud, happy to claim your salary and ask for that future promotion, your colleague can't wait to work on another project with you. How can you hold yourself accountable with more compassion in life?

Allow yourself to have fun. Something happens on the journey to womanhood, where either in a heartbeat or slowly, we stop having fun. Why would you not allow yourself to have fun? Of course, there's a time and a place, but when did you start thinking that you are unworthy or too busy for fun? Play is just as important for us grown-ups, it's through play that we release all those beautiful endorphins and feel-good vibes, it's also how you create a space that others feel safe to have fun in too. Mothering yourself to have fun may be the most important thing you can do. You may have made the decision, or sadly the decision may have been made for you, to not have children. If this is the case think of someone you know raising little people, after safety they most want their children to be happy and healthy, so they do activities that make the children happy. Your childhood may have not allowed you to have fun, especially if you had strict parents or you needed to be the sensible one. Allow yourself to have fun now, mother your inner child and find ways to play that bring you joy. Either seemingly childish play like jumping in puddles or a more grown-up way like a fun day out, something that makes you squeal with excitement and laughter. Life doesn't have to be so serious all the time.

Self-care. I bang on about this a lot, self-care isn't selfish, you can't pour from an empty cup – all those sayings and quotes are true. You're not a martyr when you forgo your own care, you are a hindrance. Harsh I know. When you deplete your resources, when you skip the things that refresh and restore you, you start to become an empty shell.

I'm not saying skipping a face mask on a Sunday night makes you a lesser person, I am talking about those pro-longed periods of time where you make conscious choices to not drink water, or eat a few veggies, you don't allow yourself to rest or do the things that puts a spark in your eyes. Admit it, you know the times I am talking about, when your priorities are off, you stop enjoying life, you don't have the energy to fake interest in the people around you, you're in a rut of false priorities. No one that really cares about you wants to see you not partaking in self-care – screw the laundry, go have a bath or glass of wine, sit down to drink a cup of hot coffee for a change. These small plentiful acts will re energise you, you will slowly return to who you really are. Your family, friends, and peers will thank you for it. When you take care of yourself, you take care of all of us. If you are struggling to recognise this in yourself, or you are trying to justify why chores are more important than you, think about someone you know who struggles to fill their own cup, are they present? Are they cherishing moments and people around them? No, they're not! So go have the goddamn bubble bath already. You would never expect your iPhone to work speedily without ever charging it, you don't let it sit at 2% being slow and unresponsive, don't do the same to the beautiful body you call home. Return to yourself.

Explore your interests and hobbies. As a child you may have been annoyed about all the extracurricular activities that your parents had you enrolled in, try not to be too mad, they were creating opportunities for you to explore your passions, to see what ignited that fire of yours. Revisit this notion, find your singing voice, sign up for the sewing club or dance school, experience a combat sport or golf, try absolutely anything that you ever briefly thought looked cool.

How would you nurture her if you were the mother of little you?

Inner Child activities

Give yourself permission to play and have fun, try a few, or all, of these:

Jumping in puddles
Playing with bubbles
Making a mess
Laughing uncontrollably
Being silly
Having a blanket day
Building a fort
Dancing without restriction
Wearing trainers if you live in formal outfits
Playing the same games you did as a child
Making mistakes
Hugging everyone
Ordering the biggest dessert for breakfast
Wearing the brightest outfit and admire it throughout the day
Letting yourself act and feel weird
Crossing the room in a silly way
Having a nap
Being radically honest
Singing at the top of your voice
Spinning around
Inviting a friend to play with you
Crafting using your imagination

Affirmation for Health

I am not sick; I am healing.
My body is a beautiful, magnificent, self-healing vessel.
I may have an illness; the illness is not my identity.
I worship my body by gifting myself with an abundance
of nutrients.
I will drink my damn water.
I am radiant.

Shadow work

The word "personality" derives from the Greek word "persona", which means mask.

We all wear a mask, it's an age-old fact, and it's getting worse. Social media has created a new norm, it's become ok to fake a personality or lifestyle. Now so many people are migrating from their true self, to play this role, thinking that this fake person is how the world wants them to show up. The whole world is so open and accessible that it is easy to gain insight into the performance of others, and in effect emulate the behaviours you perceive as attractive or endearing, suppressing any traits that you feel may not suit the narrative.

This runs a lot deeper than this new generation of social media, as we know from the inner child work, this suppressing characteristic stems from an early age. Unfortunately, this can put you out of whack, how utterly fucking exhausting it is to play a role rather than embrace the authentic you.

Shadow work is not the darkness in us, it's not the villain or the evil. The shadow is the part of you that needs more love and attention, it's your inner child and unhealed trauma. The Shadow is your blind spot – the behaviours you do not see, as you work so hard to mask with the opposite. Your shadow can sometimes be how you leave people feeling through your own projections.

Shadow work at its finest is radical self-acceptance.

Be open minded here, as it can be quite triggering and take a moment to accept. Think about your dominant traits, your shadow, the part you suppress is the opposite. You may suppress due to fears that you won't be accepted if you display them, or you may not have been allowed to express them as a child, or you mask these behaviours with a different trait to suit your environment and it has become a habit.

Here's some opposites to explore, heads up I was triggered when I first came across this theory. I was disdainful about my opposite, it took some time to respect and acknowledge, so try not to rush or dismiss. You may prefer to return to this after some thought...

Your trait	The shadow
Disciplined/hard working	Lazy work/shy
Happy	Sad
Quiet	Loud
Outspoken	Reserved
Funny	Boring/serious

I was known as hard working, always on the go and getting the results in, particularly in my working life. I always believed this to be a great trait, yet what was I hiding? No, I wasn't lazy. Shadow work is trash. This won't work for me. Ah ha-ha, I revisited some months later. Ok actually I have a tendency to be a little lazy, and so yes, I can see I forced this hard work ethic onto myself to compensate, and yes, looking back I would often project onto those around me. I would project onto peers on group projects or team members. I was holding them against the same standard I had set myself, yet my expectation was from a place of fear. If I didn't work hard, I wouldn't be validated or recognised, if I didn't work hard, I may not have the financial security I craved. I kept myself busy so I could ignore my wounded inner child, fuck addressing that ol' mess, best to keep running full speed down this track. Safer, this way I will be validated, seen as a person of authority, which I enjoyed as it meant I had control of the situation, and I had financial

144

security that wasn't always there throughout my childhood. I would get angry at "lazy" people. The lazy trait was actually something I envied, it wasn't even laziness... I was triggered at their comfort of not feeling they have to fight for control or stability, or to prove themselves. In accepting my hidden trait, I could do the work.

Using radical honesty, write down your most leading traits and explore the opposite. Journal why you so strongly avoid feeling that emotion or behaviour, get deep with it.

Shadow work triggers

Triggers for your shadow stem down to unmet needs as a child, such as:
I felt... unheard, disrespected, unsafe, unloved, blamed, responsible, left out, unwanted, unworthy, unimportant, like an imposter, betrayed, manipulated, forgotten, unseen, ignored, lonely, lied to, vulnerable, powerless, the butt of the joke, gossiped about, restricted, trapped, scolded, guilty, unlikable, unfair.

Doing the work

The next chapter will help you really dive into your shadow work, before you go, become familiar with ways you can navigate this area of healing. Notice if you relate to certain books or tv characters. Why do you empathise with them? Do the characters have the same coping mechanisms, triggers, childhood, or reactions? Prepare yourself.

Truthfully understanding your triggers and unhealed wounds can be very daunting and may mean revisiting painful memories. Remember you may wish to lean on a professional to hold your hand through this.

What to expect after:

You'll notice you treat yourself with more acceptance, and greater kindness.

You'll naturally be less judgy.

A deeper sense of contentment.

Radical self-acceptance.

You will lead an authentic and peaceful life.

A greater understanding of how to find alignment.

Improved self-awareness.

Confidence to set healthy boundaries.

Knowledge of how to break cycles of bad relationships.

You will find it easier to recognise other people's hurt without absorbing it as your own.

Greater compassion for those who project, as well as for the people who raised you.

Inner peace.

Release resentment you've been holding on to.

Empower your traits, without your subconscious sabotaging them.

You will start to see the villains in stories as people with unhealed trauma.

Hold onto your butt, it's about to get rough. Be kind to yourself throughout.

> *"Go out in the rain, you're gonna get wet"*
> – Chris Granite.

Actually I believe it was said in a film first, but Chris always says it during sparring. It is completely true, what did you expect? To spar and not get hit?

Sometimes the outcome is directly relatable to the situation you put yourself in, harsh words babe, I know. But what did you think was going to happen? How do you recognise your destructive behaviour? Do you like the comfort of these icky feelings? We find comfort in the chaos we grew up with, even when we dislike it. Shadow work shines a light on the areas in which we gravitate towards toxic or self-destructive behaviour.

Exploring your shadow.

Practice radical honesty here. Write your answers down in the form of a list, or in the style of journaling for greater clarity. Try not to rush your answers. You can choose to explore one question every few days to really explore your thoughts. This can be overwhelming, take a break whenever you need, for as long as you need.

What lies do you tell yourself?

Think of a person who triggers you – do you have similar traits?

If you could say one thing to someone who hurt you, what would it be?

How do you judge others? It's a reflection.

How do you judge yourself?

When you feel hurtful emotions, what value has been conflicted? Don't feel safe, trusted, respected, valued, wanted etc.

How do you see yourself?

How do you show yourself to others?

What do you project onto others?

Are you a victim of trauma? Have you healed?

What do you distract yourself from?

How do you distract yourself?

What do you repress?

What emotion are you addicted to?

What emotion do you avoid feeling?

What bothers you about other people?

What don't you like about yourself – not physically?

What unhealthy habits do you have?

What labels have you been given by others?

What expectations have been placed on you?

How to make it easier:

Hydrate.
Journal.

Meditate.

Be with friends, have them ask you the tough stuff.

You can lean on therapists.

Be slow and mindful with the whole process.

Sit with your feelings, you can't push it back down, analyse and observe without emotion. Allow yourself to release and heal.

Practice self-care.

Be brutally honest.

Take breaks.

Watch memories as a witness, not the main star.

Have a reboot music playlist to revive you.

Partake in inner child play during this process.

Be comfy and ready to roll into bed exhausted.

Use affirmations.

Be forgiving, recognise everyone has their own trauma.

Know that this isn't about changing you, it's about embracing and accepting yourself.

REFLECTION CHECK IN

Use daily or weekly

HIGHS	CHALLENGES	LIFE LESSONS
EVENTS	THOUGHTS	SELF CARE
GRATITUDE	DO MORE	DO LESS
DOODLES	LIKE TO REMEMBER	ACT OF KINDNESS

Take a break and some time to journal at a higher level, use this as a form of self care. The sheet can be used daily or weekly.

Manifesting magic

Manifest Your Magic

Manifestation is using your thoughts and your energy to create your reality.

"What you think you become," – Buddha.

If you are constantly feeling negative and convinced only bad things are happening to you, that is what you are focussing more on and subsequently will attract or be more aware of bad things.

On the other hand, if you can foster a more positive mindset focussed on gratitude and happiness you will start to notice more and more happy positive things in your life.

That's not to say there won't be bad things in life – toxic positivity is equally as dangerous as living in sadness. Denying thoughts and feelings can lead to greater problems (as discussed lots in this book) – suppressing and not facing your problems can lead to physiological problems. It is always important to deal with your feelings and reach out for help when you need it. Emotional trauma often manifests in the body as a disease, so it is always important to seek healing for your mind first and foremost.

How do I start to manifest?

Firstly, you need to find out what you truly desire. Ask yourself some questions.

Do I really and truly want this?

How will it improve my life?

Will it be good for me and for others?

When I picture myself having this, does it feel right?

These questions are important to ensure what you are manifesting is for the greater good.

Decide what you want – completely and fully connect with it – see it, feel it, taste it, and fully believe you will receive it.

Ensure these are realistic and achievable things. Start with something small, like a parking space in a notoriously difficult to find area, or a cup of coffee. Now dream very big! Do not place limitations on yourself but also make sure what you choose to manifest is achievable and therefore believable to you – otherwise the next step will not work.

You must TRULY and COMPLETELY believe in the thing you are manifesting.

Find out what has been holding you back.

If this is something you really want, why don't you already have it? It's important to acknowledge and deal with anything that could be holding you back.

Some of the most common things that can be stopping you from manifesting are:

Having negative beliefs

If you are constantly focussed on bad things, speaking to yourself in a negative way or expecting the worst, you simply won't be able to attract great things in your life.

It is important to practice self-care – meditation, stress relief, exercise, being in nature; whatever brings you peace and a positive mindset – DO IT!

Timing

Sometimes it's purely a case of waiting. Know that everything you want will happen, at the right time. If something isn't happening for you right now it doesn't mean that it won't – stay positive and keep believing in yourself and your goals.

Awareness

Manifesting works, but you need to too. Let's say you are manifesting a cake. You might get the eggs and flour, not the finished article. It is up to you to mix the ingredients and bake it. Your energy and efforts should match your desires.

Your Tribe

Ensure no one around you is holding you back. Free yourself from toxic people who don't believe in you, that always criticise you, or don't agree with and fully support what you are trying to achieve. They will hold you back and keep you from achieving your goals. Distance yourself from anyone who is not aligned with your goals, or simply do what you need to in order to protect yourself from their views.

Manifesting is a very personal thing, and it might take some time to find out what techniques really suit you. It really varies depending on how you feel you can best communicate with your subconscious.

You can choose to use visualisation, self-hypnosis, meditation, and any other way you that aids you in being able to convince yourself on a subconscious level that these things are yours.

Vision Boards

A very accessible and easy starting point is to create a vision board. These are particularly useful if you are a very visual person who learns best by looking. Collect images of the things you are manifesting and add them to a board. There are vision board apps, or you can get creative and make a collage.

I personally love to make little (actually BIG) changes to things like the numbers on my bank account – I blur out the figures and put in what I would like. I have holidays, dream homes, and fitness goals on a vision board saved in my phone – every now and then I look back at the board and am pleasantly surprised by things I have either achieved or made progress towards.

Self-Hypnosis and Visualisation

Using whatever technique suits you best, access a meditative state. Feel calm and relaxed and able to access your subconscious mind. Take some time to really see yourself living the life you have manifested. Really step into the future and see, feel, hear, and taste every detail. Visualisation is an extremely useful tool in many ways; it is used by successful sportspeople and businesspeople to achieve their best by completely believing in themselves. Removing any doubts or self-limiting beliefs and see and feel success. If you haven't already, check out the limiting beliefs chapter in this book, as well as completing the self-discovery questions.

3-6-9 method

Every morning repeat your desire 3 times, then you say as "I am finding" it 6 times, followed by "I have" 9 times. Let's say you are manifesting 10 new clients, 3 times you say I want 10 new clients, 6 times you say I am finding 10 new clients, followed by 9 times saying I have 10 new clients.

5x55

For 5 days, write your desires 55 times, living daily as if you already have it in your life.

Symbols

A great way to tap into the subconscious and embed the seeds of a goal for manifestation is by producing a sigil (pronounced sidg-ul). A sigil is a symbol drawn to represent a desired goal. By producing a symbol to represent your goal rather than writing it out in words you are bypassing the analytical part of the brain which is more vulnerable to limiting beliefs.

How to create your sigil:

1. Write down your goal, for example, "I can backflip"

2. List the first letters from each word – ICB

3. Draw these letters overlaying to create an abstract symbol

4. Focus on the symbol you have drawn, projecting intense feelings of love and happiness – this is to charge the symbol and place energy and intention within it.

5. Now either put the sigil away or place it somewhere you will glance at it occasionally, without concentrating consciously on it. The idea being that it is imprinted in the subconscious, therefore working its way into your belief systems free of conscious "I can't" limiting beliefs.

6. Keep the meaning of your sigil to yourself.

Top Tips for Manifesting

As with affirmations, you need to believe you already have these things – speak to your subconscious in the present tense. You deserve and are worthy of having everything you desire.

Believe in yourself, *like attracts like* – your positivity will attract more positive and great things to you.

Visit your desires before and after bed.

Finally, always recognise and appreciate when the universe has provided!

This might not seem important once you have what you desire, but it is key to achieving future manifestations. Take time to appreciate the powerful effects on manifestation. Feel thankful. Think back to when these things were just a dream, recognise how these great things have come to you. The more you see and believe in the power of manifestation, the more power it will hold for you in future.

Always share your success with others, spread positive energy, keep a gratitude journal, and record what you have manifested. Keep the positivity flowing and attract more!

Still not sure?

Putting your faith in the universe to provide can be challenging, especially if you are in the early stages of your journey towards achieving Inner Glow. So, what can you do if you aren't ready to believe in this concept wholeheartedly?

Look at it on a local level – we've covered the mind body connection. We've explored how stress and trauma can manifest as physical ailments. So, it stands to reason that we can also manifest positive outcomes using the power of our minds.

"Where attention goes – energy flows."

By simply placing our attention on something, by thinking positive thoughts and feeling positive feelings, we can create new neurological connections in our brains. Literally rewiring our thinking and re-inventing our lives. The more we focus on our strengths, on speaking kindly to ourselves, and silencing self-doubt, then the more we will be equipped to achieve greatness.

6 Signs you are finding inner peace.

You create time to reflect.
You no longer react to everything.
You are forgiving of yourself and others.
Greater connection to your body.
Treating yourself with increased compassion.
Finding joy in every day.

Imagine a woman who embodies spirituality, a woman who honours her body as the sacred temple of the spirit of life. Who breathes deeply as a prayer of gratitude for life itself. You are that woman – source unknown

Affirmation for Confidence

I move from a place of authenticity.
I own my vibe.
I embrace my flaws and charms.
I honour my voice.
I know my worth.
I am enough.
My body radiates confidence.
I am a great friend.
My friends cherish me.

Inner Glow, now you know.

At the start of this book, we invited you to track your inner glow score. Retake the test and then after you can compare to your previous results, we would love to hear your before and after scores. You can share them with Jo and I, on our social pages, or via email.

Rate yourself out of 10, be honest, use the first number that comes to mind. Try not to be influenced by the score you would like, or the score you would like others to believe. Practise radical honesty with yourself.

0 is strongly disagree, 5 is neutral, 10 is strongly agree

I understand spirituality
I have a spiritual practise
I feel grateful
I feel present
I feel aligned
I am happy
I am calm
I like my life
I have a purpose
I am in love with my life
I value experiences and connections
I feel connected to others
I feel connected to the world around me
I know how to manage my stress
I recognise where my life needs more attention/compassion

I feel connected to my body
I am in tune with my thoughts and emotions
I know how to relax my thoughts
I rarely feel stressed
I rarely feel anxious

Score /200

Thank you so much for reading Inner glow. I dream that it has helped you connect to your higher self, and unravelled your truth, so that you can find the inner peace you deserve. Own your radiant beauty, your unique charms, your quirks and embrace your flaws. Invest time into yourself and anything that inspires you or brings you joy. Set and maintain your healthy boundaries and release anything that no longer serves you. Stand up for what you know to be right and honour your inner voice.

Revisit this book in tough times, when life starts weighing you down, or those times you are feeling lost. Share Inner Glow with the other women in your life, your friends, wives, girlfriends, sisters, and mothers. Nurture the next generation with the information and empowerment we were not gifted with. Spread the warmth of totally owning who you are and being blissfully peaceful about it.

Big love
Gem

I would love to hear about your favourite parts of the book reach out at social pages here Gemstowerbooks and @Gem or by email at gem@zengemyoga.com